Need for the Bike

Paul Fournel

Need for the Bike

Translated and
with an introduction
by Allan Stoekl

University of Nebraska Press, Lincoln and London

Publication of this book was assisted by a grant from the National Endowment for the Arts. ❧

Cet ouvrage, publié dans le cadre d'un programme d'aide à la publication, bénéficie du soutien du Ministère des Affaires étrangères et du Service Culturel de l'Ambassade de France aux Etats-Unis. This work, published as part of a program of aid for publication, received support from the French Ministry of Foreign Affairs and the Cultural Services of the French Embassy in the United States.

Library of Congress Cataloging-in-Publication Data
Fournel, Paul, 1947–
[Besoin de vélo, English]
Need for the bike / Paul Fournel ; translated and with an introduction by Allan Stoekl.
p. cm.
ISBN 0-8032-2019-7 (cl. : alk. paper) — ISBN 0-8032-6909-9 (pbk : alk. paper)
1. Cycling — Anecdotes. 2. Tour de France (Bicycle race) — Anecdotes. I. Title.
GV1043.F6813 2003
796.6'2 — dc21
2003043447

The appendix, 'Sur le Tour de France 1996' (pp. 161–236 of the French original), has been omitted from this English-language edition.

Contents

Translator's Introduction

Paul Fournel's *Need for the Bike* is like no other work on cycling that I know. It's not a technical manual, not a hagiography of a few racers. The focus is not on machinery nor on heroes whose very virtue is that they cannot be emulated.

Instead Fournel presents a world, a very personal one, whose axis is the bicycle. It's a world of communication, of connection, where all people and things pass by way of the bike.

Learning to ride, Fournel makes clear, is learning to speak a language. Cycling is not simply a series of techniques but rather a descriptive universe – colorful, lyrical, peopled with gods and demons – a coherent universe in which one lives, or wants to live, and from which, on occasion, one senses a bitter exile. The Witch with Green Teeth (in English, we say 'bonking'), the Man with the Hammer ('hitting the wall'), the Wool Eaters ('wheel suckers'), Squirrels ('trackies'), and all the other locutions are first and foremost personifications of states of cyclist being. Entering this world is more than just learning slang along with a few tricks: it's fashioning and defining oneself, in opposition, in cooperation, in connection, in body and mind. The Man with the Hammer may be waiting to strike just around the next corner, but he is to be found first within the cyclist himself. Learning to ride is learning to recognize that Man and oneself through that Man: his meaning in all senses, intellectual, moral, physical.

Fournel's world is beautiful, one of landscapes, animals, people, sights, smells, and 'sensations.' And communication. The cyclist communicates with and through his body, with himself through his own body language, and finally with others through a language conditioned, even determined, by his riding. The rider is a writer, and just as his thoughts are profoundly physical when he's on a bike, so too off the bike his thoughts, shaped, formed, and deformed by the rhythm and effort of the ride, come to the fore in the writing of texts: stories, articles, poems. It's a world of writing and riding; Fournel himself says 'my work and my leisure.' But which is which? Writing ('work'?), the important writing, itself is the after-effect of riding, and riding ('leisure'?) cannot be conceived outside of the narrated world: legends, friends' stories, personal adventures of all kinds. The bicycle is the key to the past, the trigger of the earliest memories, not only of childhood enchantment but also of subliminal, physical traces that refuse analysis or definition. It is also the key to the future: one's future as a cyclist, to be sure, and hence one's relation to one's own aging body, but also to one's friends and to all of society – the countryside, the city, the world.

* * *

Given all this, the translator's task is formidable. I have, of course, always tried to convey the meaning of the French slang. In some cases this can be done only by translating it literally; one could not understand, for example, the implications of 'going to meet the Man with the Hammer' if the term were simply translated into American slang (which would be the rather flat 'hitting the wall').

On occasion this results in a mutant language that will enable the English-speaking reader to enter into the conceptual world of the French cyclists. Perhaps theirs is a richer lingo than our own; after all, the Eskimos are said to have fifteen different words for snow, and it should not be surprising, with the richness of the cycling tradition of the French that their bicycle lexicon is complex and dramatic.

In addition, Paul Fournel's prose is informed by the vast and subtle research he has carried out for more than thirty years with the Oulipo group in France. This group, whose membership has included such major writers as Raymond Queneau, Harry Mathews, Georges Perec, and Jacques Roubaud, concerns itself with all aspects of text generation: rhetoric, games, puzzles, formal rules, and the texts derived through them. Much of the most innovative and important literature of the past forty years has come from Oulipo members; though Fournel would perhaps not consider *Need for the Bike* to be a full-blown Oulipo project, its meditations on language, naming, and writing clearly are inseparable from those of Oulipo.

I've decided not to encumber the text with footnotes; instead, here are a few books that, if consulted, will provide both knowledge and pleasure. All of the works here listed are in English.

On Oulipo:

Oulipo Compendium. Edited by Alistair Brotchie and Harry Mathews. New York: Atlas Press, 1998.

Oulipo: A Primer of Potential Literature. Edited by Warren Motte. Lincoln: University of Nebraska Press, 1986.

Both of these Oulipo works contain a number of experimental writings by authors mentioned in *Need for the Bike*; the second title contains some interesting text-generation experiments by Paul Fournel.

Some works in translation by major Oulipo authors are:

Fournel, Paul. *Little Girls Breathe the Same Air as We Do*. Translated by Lee Fahnestock. New York: G. Braziller, 1979.

Mathews, Harry. *The Sinking of the Odradek Stadium*. Manchester: Carcanet, 1985.

Perec, Georges. *A Void*. Translated by Gilbert Adair. London: Harvill, 1994.

Queneau, Raymond: *Exercises in Style*. Translated by Barbara Wright. New York: New Directions, 1981.

Roubaud, Jacques. *The Great Fire of London: A Story with Interpolations*. Translated by D. Di Bernardi. Normal IL: Dalkey Archive Press, 1991.

A useful book for getting up to speed on the history of the Tour de France, many of whose major figures are mentioned by Fournel, is:

Fife, Graeme. *Tour de France: The History, the Legend, The Riders*. New York: Mainstream, 2001.

Finally, the best cycle-touring book, which includes tours of many of the places visited in *Need for the Bike*, is:

Dillon, Sally, et. al., *Lonely Planet: Cycling France*. Oakland CA: Lonely Planet, 2001.

I'd like to thank above all Paul Fournel himself, whose careful scrutiny (and corrections) of this translation have helped me greatly, and of course Nan, Bruno, and Ricky, who made valuable suggestions, all the while putting up with my endless muttering, in French cycling slang, at the dinner table. I'd also like to thank my friends Peter Starr and Jeff Wallen for their support, enthusiasm, and useful suggestions.

This translation is dedicated to the memory of my dear friend Epi Melopoulou.

Need for the Bike

There is a faster man. Maurice Leblanc, *Voici des ailes*

For my friend Louis, riding in the blue.

For the Baron, Chacha and Mado, Rémy,
Sébastien, Rino, Jean-Noël, Plaine, Jacques,
Jean-Loup, Jean, Titch, Furnon, Madel, Philippe,
for Jean-Louis, for Daniel, for Marc, for Denis,
for Ernest, for Harry, for Claire, for Jean-Emmanuel,
for Christian . . . And for all those who set out before
and whom I've forgotten.

The Violent Bike

Longchamp

I remember the dog very well. It was a yellow dog, a boxer. I remember I was the last to see him alive because I was the one who hit him.

At the same moment, I felt my front wheel give way and my handlebars twist against my left arm. I felt the breeze from the *peloton*, opening up and yelling all around me, and then I woke up, sitting on the Longchamp sidewalk, trying to scratch my phone number in the sand, in case I passed out again.

There was the first hospital, where they found my arm too messed up for them; there was the badly sprung ambulance that shook me up; there was Boucicaut hospital and the emergency service.

It was three o'clock, and my morning ride was already taking a big bite out of the afternoon.

My arm by now was calm in its splint.

The surgeon had told me: 'You've lost some bone; we're going to have to screw plates on and do a graft with bone from your hip,' and he went off to lunch. I was just about to finish digesting the cereal bar I had had during my circuit before coming to the surgery unit.

At exactly this point there were five of them riding at the front, and I had the sense that the great Demeyer was taking cover. On the cobbles he was circumspect; he was riding strongly, as always, but at the back. Moser and De Vlaeminck weren't doing much better. Hinault, for his part, was pulling the train with his teeth clenched, as on any other hard day. Paris-Roubaix isn't a race where you joke around; his world champion's jersey was filthy, the kind of filth you frame under glass. The closeups on TV showed him tight-faced, concentrating hard. He wasn't trying to make a break, and nothing was more exasperating than watching him carrying everybody in his panniers on the way to Roubaix.

They were ten Ks from the finish line when the surgeon came back:

'Let's go – the operating room's ready.'

'Five minutes . . . I want to see the end of the race.'

'You'll find out about it later.'

'I won't be able to sleep if I don't know.'

'With what they're going to give you that would surprise me.'

He made the mistake of glancing at the TV, and he had to sit down on the edge of my bed. The race's tension was so extreme that he didn't say a word.

Kuiper entered the velodrome first, with De Vlaeminck, pallid, on his wheel. Four hundred meters from the line, the Badger (Hinault) took the lead and upped the pressure. Demeyer tried to whip past him but couldn't get beyond his pedals. Nobody else had the strength to try.

The Badger picked up his bouquet and publicly restated that the race was, indeed, bullshit. Now he knew exactly what he was talking about.

Then there was my first shot, the gurney, the green smock, the second shot. Sitting on the operating table, in a contented haze, I did an inventory of the tools that were gleaming next to my bed: nails, screws, casts, pliers, a saw . . .

There was a Black and Decker drill, and I went under sorry that it wasn't a Peugeot . . . Great team, Peugeot.

Saint-Julien

That wasn't my first test.

Every cyclist, even a beginner, knows that at any moment in his life he could have a rendezvous with a door. It could open in front of him at any time, from the right, the left, at the moment he least expects it, at a bend in the street, at an intersection, right in the middle of a straight and clear road.

As an urban cyclist, I have a complete collection: right doors, left doors, high truck doors, low convertible doors, all accompanied by a range of reactions, from the extremely rare 'Excuse me' to 'You should have been more careful' and the colorful 'You scratched my paint.' At a reasonable speed this encounter ends in a fractured finger, an injured shoulder, a persistent headache, a wide and dangerous swerve into a busy street.

I had the honor of being initiated into this cycling discipline at a very early age, and I was awarded my first car door at the very beginning of my career. I was coming back from an insignificant outing with my cousins, and I was riding carefully on the right, as I had been taught. We were coming back at a good clip because it was already apéritif time.

The door opened in front of me with no discernible hesitation. My bike stayed on one side, and I went flying over it, in a single mass – I wasn't yet using toe-clips. I landed without subtlety on the other side, head first into the gravel. Half my face was pitted with little dirty bits of stone. I could feel my lips and an eyebrow swelling. I was one-eyed, mute. Could even my own mother recognize me?

The lady who had caught me off guard was highly embarrassed, given my tender years. She took me in her arms and carried me into her yard, while trying to invent all possible solutions to efface this nasty moment from our two lives. First and foremost she wanted to make sure that nothing was broken; she seemed to be trying to count my bones, one by one. 'I didn't do it on purpose,' she assured me, and I was perfectly convinced of this because I could think of a thousand other, more efficient, methods you could use to kill your small neighbors. I started to think she was muddle-headed and got impatient waiting for my mom.

That's when the lady had the brilliant idea of bringing me a big glass of Martini to bring me around. I gulped it down and immediately, after my first door, got my first major buzz. The lady leaned over my swollen head; her cheeks were fat and I wanted to slap them. I was perfectly drunk, perfectly smashed-up, perfectly violent, and my one and only wish was to get back on my bike.

The Back Road

At the end of the Tour de France, summer reached its sad point: long, infernally hot afternoons with nothing particularly glorious to be interested in.

Fortunately there was still the prospect of the next cycling Grand Prix of our village, when we would pass spare wheels to the riders and, in front of our house, give them water bottles.

I was ten, I had a green bike, and I got ready for the event as if I were a racer myself. My physical training consisted of a series of crazy sprints on the road that went from our house to the village. In those days the road was deserted, and I could sweep from left to right without any risk to André Darrigade, my major sprinting rival, against whom I pulled out all the stops in the last three hundred meters, while the courageous and powerful Roger Hassenforder chased us with his tongue lolling ten lengths behind. As a general rule I crossed the line, which was right in front of our door, with my arms up, the victor. Sometimes, when the competition was too intense, I had to rock the bike back and forth to the final centimeters to win by a tire; other times I lost by a hair and pounded the top of my bars with my fists, demanding a rematch.

That afternoon the confrontation was terrible. It was horribly hot, and we were sprinting hard in the dust and sun. My throat was on fire, and my muscles were strained. I have to admit that since I was rather chubby my muscles were sorely tested. So I had to do this final sprint in a blind, total rush, an all-out effort with my back bent and my head scrunched down into my shoulders.

When, with a final groan, I raised my head to make sure I had really won, I saw the enormous lady right in front of me, a few centimeters away. It was too late to try anything, too late even to brake, and we crashed into each other with an enormous explosion of fruits and vegetables.

My front wheel managed to ram right into hers, tire against tire, and we bounced off each other. The crates she had mounted on her carrier, the bread and wine she was lugging in the shopping bag hanging from her handlebars – all of it was scattered on the road. She was planted there on her butt, black dress bunched around her knees, bun drooping over her ear. I blew very hard on my burning knee; I blew very hard on my scraped elbow. She simply asked me what I was doing on this side of the road, which was her side of the road. With my head down, I absolutely insisted on picking up every eggplant and squash, reattaching every bungee cord, before limping back home to cry, finally.

L'Ance

After some debate, we decided to bring along the girls. We were going to have a picnic alongside the river, and their presence seemed indispensable, at least to the older ones among us.

The ladies were perched on squeaky and greaseless contraptions set up for shopping or going to the beach. One barely straddled her big sister's bike, and the other had her knees bobbing up to her shoulders as she tried to ride her little brother's two-wheeler. Our team resembled anything but a *peloton*. It was fun for a while, but then time started to drag. At this pace, our picnic was going to turn into a late lunch, then dinner, and finally even a night under the stars, with all the parental problems that implied.

So we tried to pick up the pace by setting up relays. We were going to push the ladies in the right spot, enable them to climb the hills with a little more ardor.

I ended up with the dense one. Full of good will but dense. She understood perfectly well that this whole scenario was intended to help her, and grateful, she tried to help in return. At the exact moment I was to take my turn and give her a vigorous push on the derrière, she had the idea of generously saving me the effort by standing up and pushing on the pedals. My hand encountered nothing but air, and my momentum plunged me into the void.

By an alchemy well known to cyclists, tiny useful objects one sees on the best bikes are easily turned into formidable weapons when the situation gets complicated. This time, it was the harmless shift lever that turned itself into a blade and planted itself into my right thigh.

My buddies carried out a very technical rotation of my bike in the air and pulled the steel out of the wound. Blood flowed, and little fat particles appeared. It all seemed to call for a few stitches.

The doctor greeted me with exasperation: 'Again!' he gravely observed. 'I'm getting sick of your goofing off. I see you with your buddies in town. For the inconvenience, I'm going to sew you up – don't you move for three weeks! – but I'm going to do the stitches without anesthesia. That'll teach you!'

And that's what he did. He was a genuine country doc.

Longchamp

That summer I flatted twenty-three times. Thanks to inflating and reinflating my tires in the ditches and on the hills, my arms were thicker than my thighs. My tubular budget had burst insanely, and the absolutely last one I was willing to buy was in place under my saddle. It was too new, bought on the run, and cheap. It's a general rule that one never takes a new sew-up on a ride: it hasn't been stretched, it doesn't have the precious residue of glue, and it's difficult to mount.

When, after twenty Ks, my front tire, put on the day before, went flat, thanks to an honest enough thumb tack, I jumped off the bike in a hurry and regretfully put on my last little tire. I put it on without fresh glue, on a badly prepared rim: it was the big mistake you make because the twenty-fourth flat is one too many; because, when you're going fast, suddenly stopping is just not acceptable; because, when the gang keeps riding and you have to catch up, every second is paid for with pain in your thighs; because flatting is not what a cyclist does.

Stretching the new sew-up – which always seems too small – putting it on by pressing the wheel against my chest, inflating it, putting the wheel back on, cost me six kilometers of chasing, my nose on the handlebars, my eyes filled with sweat and my right shoulder in a cramp. The badly mounted tire was suffering from a little bulge near the valve, and it made a bumping noise, 'tock,' every time it went around. I felt it in my hands and shoulders. Luckily there were some flat sections on the road, and I had the *peloton* in my sights.

Of course, afraid of being left stranded, I came back to the group too quickly, as one often does when one is anxious to get back in the shelter of the line. I arrived seriously winded at the very moment they decided to pick up the pace.

Having to get off my ass exactly when I really needed to recuperate was sheer torture – one could let go for less. Nevertheless I stood up on the pedals, resigned to more quad burn. What was going on at the front seemed to be getting serious, and the more exhausted guys started to fall back. Fighting fire with fire, I decided to go for it and got down in the drops, determined to get back in. Using an old sprinter's technique, I started to rock the bike side to side, to come down on the pedals hard, machine-like. A swift glance showed me the three bike-lengths I still had in front of me, and I put my head down, eyes on the wheel, for a better aero effect.

So it was in extreme close-up that I saw my wheel tilt, the tire shoot off the rim and squash onto the road. Then I saw it twist up and jam behind the fork crown, producing the most brutal deceleration I've ever experienced. I didn't take my eyes off the knot it made at that precise location, and to this day I could still sketch it. I can see it from every angle, since I somersaulted over the handlebars and crashed flat on my back, with the bike, and that damn twenty-fourth sew-up, landing on top of me.

The road took my breath away.

That was the first time I really drowned in the tar.

San Francisco

In those days I was living in California, and I had carefully brought along two racing bikes. Once there, in San Francisco, I got hold of a used mountain bike – a local product with twenty-four speeds – that was supposed to get me up the steep streets I climbed every day on the way to work.

Californians are gentle and courteous drivers. At every intersection they have four stop signs, and they respect them, giving the right of way to the first one there (who isn't necessarily the first to arrive). As soon as they see a pedestrian they jam on the brakes with a smile and let him cross. But, simply put, they hate cyclists. You'd swear they were aiming at them. It's true that nothing in the California Highway Code tells them they shouldn't run them down. And it's also true that the tough guys and gals who survive on the San Francisco hills are real virtuosos. Be that as it may, my very first week there I found myself on the ground twice, once thanks to a driver who almost didn't see me, and another time thanks to a bus driver who had seen me quite well.

So I decided to take that worthy bus to work and save my bike for weekends and the exploration of the (magnificent) California countryside.

The next Saturday, on the climb from Stinson beach – the one you do with the Pacific Ocean at your back and the eucalyptus-covered ridge in front of you – I got to know a rustic California ditch, pushed there in a not-so-gentle way by a driver who obstinately wanted to pass me and get by an oncoming car at the same time. So I landed in the ditch, hugging my bike with my thighs and flattening myself as if I were under machine-gun fire, so as not to miss anything of the amazing spectacle of a Ford Explorer passing an oncoming Chevy Yukon.

I had just turned fifty and it seemed advisable to save my cycling urges for Golden Gate Park on Sunday morning, when it's closed to cars.

So I decided on weekdays, against the will of my quads and calves, to spin in the gym.

California gyms are open 24/7. You can work on your biceps at three in the morning and buy your Creatine at the counter. It's a place to live, and every time I went the same guy with a red headband was staring in the same mirror at the same pointlessly flexing muscles. You also saw some really good-looking hunks and babes. 'Low Impact' and 'Tae-Bo' were starting to lose their appeal, and the stationary-bike fad had been launched.

The idea is to have a *peloton* on wheel-less bikes, going nowhere. The Yellow Jersey, usually seen only from behind, sits facing you and urges you on. You climb imaginary hills with him, plunge down shady ravines, and devour endless straight lines. The ride lasts an hour, and you walk out totally beat, with swollen quads and empty eyes. The only pleasure in the whole business is the huge fan blowing a headwind at you that does you only good.

For a landscape freak like me it wasn't a terribly attractive proposition. But I decided to do it anyway, just to stay in shape.

California wants to be in the vanguard of everything, and it succeeds. So it's also in the vanguard of do-it-yourself repair. I was sitting on my saddle, ten minutes before takeoff, pedaling gently forward and back (stationary bikes make possible tricks that even trackies can't do), to warm up, when my makeshift saddle repair gave way. I fell on my back with all my (considerable) weight, my head plowing into the bike behind me. Coccyx, spinal column, skull – everyone got their money's worth.

I was so far out of it that the doctor they called had me repeat my name and count my fingers. He closed my wounds and hurried me into a howling ambulance that hurried me to the hospital.

From that point on my financial problems were paramount, and my health was secondary . . .

And still I ride.

Not one of these accidents turned me off or made me regret riding. As soon as I'm on the ground I do an inventory of the damage in order to figure out how long it'll be before I can get back on the bike. That's also the first question I ask the doctor. Then I bargain with myself. I've ridden with stitches, with bandages, with scabs. I've ridden out of focus, undefined, until the luminous clarity of being in shape returned.

I've never lacked the desire.

It's been a sunny and twisting road, from the childish desire to own a bike to the need to ride it. Up to now every time I've questioned myself, I've just jumped back on my lovely bike and gone for a spin.

Bike Desire

Stroke of Genius

The bike is a stroke of genius. On that day in the nineteenth century when Michaux put a chain and pedals on it, it had practically attained its final form. Since then they've refined the details, they've been fanatical about the subtleties, but the basics of the machine are the same.

If I compare my yellow bike from 1960 to my metallic beige bike of the year 2000, their differences are minimal. The latter is lighter by three kilos and more rigid (but not by too much), its gear shifters are in the brake levers, its saddle is made of plastic covered with leather (which might not indicate progress), the fork crown is no longer chromed. There is real progress: clipless pedals, which spare me the hard labor of adjusting the cleats under the shoes but which give the rider, when he's on foot, a duck-walk that's hardly compatible with the dignity of the pedestrian.

After forty years of riding, I've seen steel replaced by aluminum (which groaned under a standing rider), aluminum replaced by carbon fiber, carbon fiber by titanium, and titanium by steel, and on it goes.

The fork stood and straightened up only to curve again. The wheelbase got tighter, then loosened. We went from ten speeds to twenty-four.

It's easy to distinguish real progress from fashions.

These are details, certainly costly details (shaving grams ends up costing a fair amount), but they're fundamentally unimportant.

The bike is a brilliant device that permits a seated person by the force of just his or her own muscles to go twice as far and twice as fast as a person on foot.

Thanks to the bike, there is a faster man.

The bike is in itself a form of doping. Which doesn't simplify things. It's the tool of natural speed; it's the shortest path to the doubling of yourself. Twice as fast, two times less tired, twice as much wind in your face.

It's all right always to want more.

Light Weight

Sitting on the seat, not carrying the weight of one's body, makes bike riding something like swimming, something like flying. The saddle carries you along, like water, like air: it's the saddle, but also the frame, and the tires, and the compressed air in the tires that give you wings.

Still, the difference between cyclist and swimmer is that the cyclist, eyes open and hair flying in the wind, goes faster than a mere man – whereas the swimmer drags along, eyelids closed, ears plugged.

The difference between bike and flight is that the bike is possible and flight isn't, yet.

Miracle

The bike always starts with a miracle. For days you tremble, you hesitate; you tell yourself that you'll never get rid of that hand guiding you, under the seat.

My father and mother took turns holding onto me, as did, no doubt, one of my cousins, from whom I'd inherited the little bike. Whoever it was who was in charge of my miracle.

They'd taken off the training wheels, and I took to the field in front of our house and followed its slope down, gaining momentum. I was looking for the magic moment that makes the duo stay up when it should go down, and I wiped out (already) and got up again.

And then one morning I no longer heard the sound of someone running behind me, the sound of rhythmic breathing at my back. The miracle had taken place. I was riding. I never wanted to put my feet back down for fear that the miracle wouldn't happen again. I was in seventh heaven.

I did a tour around the house, proving to myself that I could do four right turns (for a number of weeks I preferred turning right). I was no longer afraid of anything. I rocketed past the clump of nettles that usually scared me; I rode panic-free down the long lonely road behind the house and came out in front again, in triumph, but still unable to raise my hand in a victory salute.

I've never gotten over this miracle.

Learning to swim didn't move me like this, and it was really only learning to read that equaled the intensity of learning to ride. Within a few months, then, I learned, in that order, riding and reading. At the age of five, that Christmas, I had arrived: I knew what my work would be, and my leisure.

Dragon Green

He was a strange uncle, a little on the heavy side, a little cockeyed. One of those guys who wear heavy suits and big dark glasses and were supposed to have managed nightclubs. They star in the family history, cruising through it in big cars that purr like cats.

He was an uncle who kept kids at a distance, and you sometimes worried about him, suspecting he was mean. Never having known him when I was an adult, I still think of him as a tough guy.

He was, however, given the role of good fairy by my father on my ninth birthday. At the time he ran a factory – where they made bikes.

He was the one, then, who had my first frame brazed and built up.

I chose the color green, like Anquetil's (who at the time was racing on a candy-green Helyett), and had it equipped with three speeds – low, medium, and high, gearing 101.

When it was ready, I went down to the factory, which remains fixed in my memory as enormous and black, shot through with sparks, inhabited by masked men whose fingers spat fire, resonating with the bright racket of tubes clinking on workbenches and the rainy patter of the sanding wheel.

It was way in the back, luminous against the dark wall, just out of its lair, 'dragon green,' and it was *my* bike.

I already knew, from having tried out a few of my older cousins' bikes, that cycling is a sport that hurts your legs, that demands extensive effort and patience, but I was unaware of four essential things that my green dragon was about to teach me:

1. When you get on your first bike you enter a language you'll spend the rest of your life learning, and you transform every move and every event into a mystery for the pedestrian.

With my hands on the hoods, my nose was down at the level of the bars. They changed the stem and the drops, adjusted the saddle-rails, raised the post to its proper height, and I was ready to spin, ready to take off like a shot, ready to break away. There I was, about to meet the Witch with Green Teeth ('bonk'), confront the Man with the Hammer ('hit the wall'), all set to jostle, eat wool in the pack ('wheel suck'), stretch out, blow up, pack it in, stick my nose to the window ('go to the front'), just itching to force my way into echelons, determined to knock down kilometer after kilometer, all in order to join the Edenic clan of the silky-smooth pedal strokers . . .

2. When you get on a bike, you enter into the history and legends that you'll discover in thousands upon thousands of copies of *L'Équipe*.

It's forging your own fork in Sainte Marie-de-Campan; it's jumping into a plane-taxi after having won the Dauphiné-Libéré to catch the nighttime start of Bordeaux-Paris; it's winning the Tour de France five times; it's droppping Merckx on the climb to Pra-Loup; it's keeping Poulidor in line on the Puy de Dôme climb; it's entering the velodrome at Roubaix, alone, for the second time; it's winning the Giro d'Italia in the blinding snow of the Gavia pass; it's, whether you like it or not, falling and refalling into the abyss at Perjuret and dying a little every time you climb the Ventoux on the Bédoin side. . .

The divine solitude of the cyclist is peopled with shadows the sun casts on the roughness of the road.

Sitting on my first saddle, I learned to feel the breath of the great cycling *peloton* of all times and places.

3. When you get on a bike, it's not to forget a machine but, on the contrary, to connect with it.

The minute I hit the climb, I glance nervously at the crankset of the guy passing me – just as I thought, he has oval chainrings and 175mm cranks!

What ecstasy does an eighth cog on the freewheel promise? How do I strip from the frame the 500 grams I put on my gut over winter?

While the ancients are still comparing the relative merits of Reynolds steel and of aluminum, the moderns are debating the stiffness of metal-matrix or the wind resistance of aero wheels.

Changing a component, repainting the frame, putting on clipless pedals – all this reproduces, forever, the happiness of the green dragon glowing deep in its lair.

4. To get on a bike is to get ahold of the landscape.

First my front wheel, then my father's legs (which are the legs I know best in the world), then the larger landscape, when I attained equilibrium and fitness.

The next day, I rode my first classic. Twenty-five kilometers of the Haute-Loire, which determined my definitive love of climbing, twenty-five kilometers of happiness which have since been devoured by freeways and vacation homes.

The next year saw my first stage race and my first major climbs. That's how I started my patient Tom Thumb labor, scattering droplets of sweat on the roads of France and the world. Mountains, plains, bushes, trees, streams, ditches, and eternal snow were hidden in my green bike – it took only some riding to learn.

Haute Couture

When I lean my bike against a wall I watch the eyes of passersby light up. Even those who don't show any signs of being cyclists stop for a moment and lean over the bike, pushing up their hats. They're ten years old, or a hundred, they're in a hurry, they have time – they always stop for a second.

The desire to have a beautiful bike is something shared by everyone. This desire comes with childhood; some cultivate it, others repress it, but it's always there.

If you discount racers, who struggle over fractions, nobody needs a really nice bike. No Sunday rider has his weight down to the last kilo. But beautiful bikes have a special virtue, cast a secret spell: they make you want to do more. Going out on an attractive bike is a pleasure in itself. You just need to see the handsome guys at Longchamp, chatting at the top of the hill, their butts planted on their pretty frames.

*　*　*

I've only owned beautiful bikes, cyclist haute couture, made to measure. I've loved all of them, even the aluminum one Jacques Balutin loaned me that screamed in pain every time I jumped on the pedals. Even my blue carbon-fiber job, whose fork was so stiff it froze up my back.

I prefer rigid but supple steel, which isn't really so heavy, and which is fun to have sanded down and repainted every two or three years.

I have to say that I'm lucky to be from Saint-Étienne, where, even up until a few years ago, beautiful bikes were turned out. I climbed up through the town the long way (it's shaped like that) to go see 'my' shop windows. I kept up with the latest stuff, checked out the workshops, harassed the shopkeepers with questions – all in preparation for my Sunday excursions.

Two or three times a year my father took me over to see Louis Nouvet. He was kind of a (red-headed) giant who seemed to have come straight from *Of Mice and Men* and who spoke in a thin voice slightly softened by a lisp. He brazed frames for the Olympus of cycling: Anquetil and Poulidor, of course, but also for the touring aristocracy, the princes of challenges and the lords of 'Flèches,' the barons of Vélocio. He was a direct competitor of Alex Singer or Jo Routens.

His 'factory,' as my father called it, was set up in a rabbit hutch deep in a poor working-class neighborhood. You could make him out from a distance, framed by the gaps between the warped boards, his black goggles on his forehead, his brazing torch in hand.

He started by taking your measurements, and he noted everything: how many kilometers a year? Fenders or no fenders? Racing, no racing? Clinchers or sew-ups? Fixed gear in winter?

However you responded, he measured the length of your legs, your waist, the length of your forearms, the size of your feet. . . . You would have thought he was ready to make you a suit.

Afterward, you had to choose the tube set (in general Reynolds or Vitus steel) as well as the lugs (cut or filed), decide on the length of the stem and the width of the bars. The saddle would be a Brooks, recut (I can still hear him saying the name in his broken English).

Then it was time to think about the inessential – the components, in other words.

My entire youth was marked by the magic name of Campagnolo. Campagnolo derailleurs, brakes, pedals, cranksets were to cycling art what Leica is to photography, what Porsche is to cars, what Laguiole is to knives. Well made, long-lasting, expensive, inevitable. Simplex and Mavic battled in vain. The 'all Campy' bike was the *nec plus ultra*. Nouvet recognized that Campy parts were expensive but that, on the word of a specialist, they were the 'sharpest around.' They still are, in spite of the Shimano vogue.

Finally you came back, for a moment, to the essential: choosing the color. Nouvet liked metallic gray. As for me, after green, I tended for quite a while to choose red, but I've also had blue with black accents, dark gray, mauve, and yellow.

Since then Nouvet has died and with him the secret of his brazing, but the ritual has stayed the same with Guy Seyve, La Sablière, Ferappy.

Styles change, but the haute couture of Saint-Étienne remains.

Machine

During every one of my childhood vacations, I was lucky enough to have my bike in my room and to be able to look at it.

I wish it were still there.

You buy a bike because it looks good; you choose it carefully, and then you sit on it and you don't see it any more.

I get more out of looking at my friends' bikes than at my own.

One of the things I enjoy is knowing that my friend Rémy rides a bike I used to own. So when I ride with him I see my old bike, and I find it pretty.

I'd like my bike to be in my room, like a sculpture, like a potentially mobile Calder. Not really hanging there but leaning against a white wall, in the sunlight from the window. It's red, it's fine, it shines. I've just changed the bar tape, and it looks new. I polished the cranks this morning and put a drop of paint on the little scratch a bit of gravel cut into the frame enamel. The scratch is completely gone.

The great Brambilla was a courageous racer who didn't pamper himself. When he felt that he hadn't been up to the job, he put his bike in his bed and slept on the floor. That probably didn't do much for his conditioning, but his outlook benefited greatly.

In those days, racers kept their bikes in their rooms mainly so they wouldn't be stolen. Riding the Tour de France is hard enough, but following the *peloton* on foot is even harder.

I've had four bikes stolen. Four city bikes, in Paris, taken from me over a span of two years. After that, Dutch-style bikes went out of fashion, and only mountain bikes were stolen. I was saved.

I went to the flea market to try to find them, but there were so many, and so many that looked alike, that I found it somewhat revolting.

It's not the same with racing bikes. Starting from a finite number of combinable elements, every rider creates his own machine, which he can recognize at a glance.

With my eyes closed I could immediately tell which of my bikes I was on. I could describe it, part by part. I know exactly how each differs from the one before it.

I've been told that pro racers don't have pretty bikes, and that they don't give a hoot. In fact they have very beautiful, very refined, and very reliable bikes, but they're often hidden, and you have to know how to distinguish them. For reasons that are easily understood, racers cruise on handmade bikes that have the paint jobs of the mass-market products. A cursory glance can give you the impression that these are bikes like those you see in shop windows or supermarkets. That's not at all the case: one bike can hide another. Technicians have told me thousands of little things about the tastes and manias of various riders (but as for the colors, no choice). Pedro Delgado, for example, liked only the aluminum frames made by the chief competitor of his sponsor, who made frames only in steel. So he used only aluminum but hidden under a steel paint-job.

It is true, though, that certain racers could care less about their machine so long as it rolls – this was often said of Anquetil. They don't even pay attention to the gears they're starting out with in the morning. They delegate the love of their bike to their mechanics – who know a thing or two about love.

Maybe I should have been a mechanic?

Gears

People are obsessed with gears: 'what did you put on?' 'What do you have?' Gearing is expressed by two numbers: the number of teeth on the front chainring and the number on the rear cog. To simplify, let's say that the higher the first number and the lower the second, the higher the gear. A 52 x 14 (you don't mention the 'x') is a gear for descents, while 42 x 22 is a gear for mountain climbing. For the Sunday rider – for me – gearing indicates two extremely important things: the grade of the road and the condition of the rider.

Cyclists in general are fascinated by big gears, to the point where you see some pedaling in slow motion on climbs for the simple pleasure of 'turning a big gear.' People are fascinated by the strong. Mind-boggling stories circulate everywhere, of gears as huge as plesiosaurs, Loch Ness monsters. In more than one guy's imagination to 'get into the big ring' is already to go fast.

One morning when the group was rolling in a forest on the other side of Versailles, one of our buddies took off. The group reacted immediately, getting down in the drops, with a whooshing of de-railleurs and shifts into the big ring. I was carefully watching Dédé Le Dissez, who was riding with us – a former pro, Poulidor's teammate, Tour stage winner, now in books. He made do with spinning faster in his little ring. I came up to him:

'You economizing on your gears, Dédé?'

– I'll shift up when it gets *really* fast.'

In 1996 when my friends learned that I was leaving to follow the Tour de France, they almost all asked me to check out the gears. It was the universal demand, the primordial concern: 'What are they running?'

Pros have the reputation of using monster gears, noted with smugness by *L'Equipe*: 54 x 11, they say, for sprinting; 44 x 19 on the climbs. All this contributes to the magic aura of the riders.

So one morning before a mountain stage I went up to one of them to ask him about the gears he was using on the climbs. He gently made fun of me: 'Special gearing for the mountains is fine for you' (He gathered I was a cyclist from my stripy tan.) 'I just use race gearing. If the race is in a big gear, so am I. If it's in a small one, I'm in one too. Ask the race what gear it'll be in on the climbs, and I'll be in it.'

Class

I've always been very attentive to my position on the bike. A good position allows you to go faster, further, longer. So it's worth lingering over.

I take measurements; I try things; I evolve my position over time, depending on the bike I'm using and the profile of the roads I'm riding. I add more measurements to my made-to-measure bikes.

In spite of these small details, I still look as awkward as a cow on a bike. It's scandalous, but that's the way it is.

There's one cycling mystery that fascinates me: some people are made to go on a bike. We say they have 'class.'

Put them on any old bike and they seem at home, superb, and finally complete.

This has nothing to do with their athletic ability – you see it among the champions but also among cycling tourists. They can't escape fatigue or the usual agony; they're simply wonderful to see. They're so beautiful that they're kind of a living lie.

Anquetil was the very model of this. Even when he was scraping bottom he seemed on parade, in cahoots with the wind, feline and unreadable.

For that's really the lie of class: you can read it only as harmony; effort leaves no trace. The racer with class never hunches over, never pedals squares, never loses it. He shows no signs of fatigue, and he collapses, magnificent and exhausted, only after you have long since given up challenging him, he seemed so at ease.

Louis Nucera was that kind of guy.

A car stole him from the cycling world, but his perfect image is still vivid. I see him climbing the Pilat, hands on the top of the bars, splendid. I see him in the valley of the Petit Morin, vying in elegance with Jean-Louis Ezine. He had the grace of those spiders that dance on the water without wetting their toes.

Mountain Bike

The desire to have a nice made-to-measure bike that evolves over time, with different adaptations, the desire to feel good on it, the desire to create it as you like – all these ensure that very quickly, like a fountain pen, the bike becomes an object you can't loan out. You can't even lend it to yourself. You specialize it, you intend it exclusively for what it does best. You certainly wouldn't lend it to yourself to go out and get crazy in the woods.

At that point you start to want another bike.

I had one just for crossing streams, an old beater, stripped of all its accessories, with coaster brakes, fat tires, and moustache handlebars. It was my bike for trails and woods, my mountain bike before they existed. It was good for everything: paths, warrens, thickets, streams, the Loire.

We crossed where it's low, where you can get across with the water only up to the hubs. Around there the current's fast and the bottom is carpeted with round stones covered with slippery weeds. The winner was whoever could get furthest before putting his foot down. The idea was to do a sort of swamped Paris-Roubaix: a flooded race with invisible and unforeseeable cobbles.

We got up speed coming down the embankment, shooting into the water with spray on both sides. Then you had to keep your balance while leaning onto one side to resist the current, and negotiate the rocks as best you could, with supple arms and your butt off the saddle.

As a general rule we managed to cover a few meters before toppling into the water, but sometimes a miracle happened and we kept going for fifteen, twenty meters . . . It seems to me nobody ever got all the way to the other side, and our efforts ended with a half-flesh, half-fish *peloton*, pushing bikes and laughing through the rushing Loire.

The bikes we used for these expeditions were old bombers originally intended for trips (to the market) with squeaky returns home. The youthful jamming we subjected them to, when they should have been enjoying their retirement, wasn't always in their best interest. Wheels tacoed, frames were toast, brake levers hung.

Mine was especially hungry for headsets. The inventors of the mountain bike were smart when they put suspension forks on it. When I was riding mine that option was out of the question, so I often ended up with my fingers stuck in red grease with little ball bearings, trying to firm the handlebars up a bit.

That klunker died a hero's death, its front wheel divorced from the frame. It was sacrificed so that my road bike could remain the gem that it was, familiar only with the sleek, gentle tar.

Paris

In Paris – for I'm also a Parisian cyclist – I use a bike that's a real regression. It possesses everything that history has removed from my road bike: fenders, mud flaps, a rack, a chain guard . . . Even though it was born a Peugeot, it has the black dignity, and weight, of a Dutch bike.

I get around about as fast as a city bus, and I cover about fifteen hundred kilometers a year. There are risks, but they can be lessened by avoiding bike lanes (outside of those set off by low dividers). It helps to have eyes all around your head and new brakes.

With those precautions, Paris is a festival of cycling. Montparnasse is a real mountain, the Champ-de-Mars is a real plain, and the Champs-Elysées is a real false flat. Claire Paulhan, Jacques Réda, Harry Mathews, with whom I ride in town, all know this quite well.

Above all I like doing stores. Bike speed requires you to be selective about what you see, to reconstruct what you sense. In that way you get to the essential. Your gaze brushes over the title of a book or a cover, a newspaper catches your eye, you glimpse a potential gift in a window, a new bread in a bakery. That's the proper speed of my gaze. It's a writer's speed, a speed that filters and does a preliminary selection.

My city bike gets me special attention. When I attend official functions I park it between the chauffeured limousines; the drivers stare at me, eyes wide open, as I ride up in a suit and tie. I even had the pleasure of a very worthy official bicycle when I was the director of the Ramsay publishing house.

One morning when I was having breakfast at Fouquet's (not really a habit of mine) with Bernard Pivot to show him our book list, he insisted on accompanying me to the sidewalk to see me get on my bike and merge into the flow of the Champs-Elysées. On my way down to the Place de la Concorde I thought about the kind of car I would have had to have in order to make the same impression.

Riding like this around Paris is my way of making sure I get an hour and a half of light, daily exercise. For sure, you have to know how to second-guess the rain, when to give it up and jump in a bus to stay presentable. For sure, sometimes you have to hold your nose and try to absorb only the minimum of oxygen necessary for the effort. For sure, sometimes you need some courage to go and visit friends who live way up in Montmartre. But there's a huge reward when you cross a bridge over the Seine when the sun is setting, or when you calmly thread your way through an endless traffic jam, smiling at the drivers who are drumming their fingers on the wheel or picking their noses.

When my daughter was small I rode her to day care on my bike. I set up a little chair on my rack and I tied her in it, using her big pink scarf. She was absolutely delighted with her morning excursion and turned around, beaming. The chair spent the day with her, and we met again in the afternoon to cruise down the rue de la Convention.

Nights in Paris are gracious. Traffic is light; the side streets are deserted and silent. You roll along to the humming of the generator. After our Oulipo meeting at Jacques Jouet's I like to ride across the city with Harry: the rue de Renard, the rue de Rivoli, the rue Bonaparte . . . I 'drop him off' along the way, on the rue de Grenelle, and continue on to the fifteenth arrondissement.

Sunday morning is gracious as well. You can ride the major thoroughfares without intimidation or danger. The streets of Paris are deserted, since all the cyclists – me included – are out in the country . . .

Maniac

A little while ago I noticed that for thirty years I had been happily mounting my bike by raising my right leg and passing it over the saddle.

Since then I do it with the right leg over, then the left.

Outfit

You have to know how to look good when you're riding. You have to impress your adversary with your elegance. To look good is already to go fast.

First you think of wearing the reigning champion's jersey, hoping that it will contain a little of his strength and that it will inspire respect in others. Then you can refine your image, give yourself a 'look': a 'bike tourist' look with shorts over your bib; a color-coordinated look with the frame; a group look to encourage teamwork . . .

Bib shorts are made of synthetic material, elastic all around, skin-tight. They go pretty far down on the thigh and include suspender-straps that hold them in place. Inside, the bottom is lined with a foam pad covered with synthetic chamois, which protects you from irritation and other irregularities.

It's the piece of equipment that has most evolved over my years of riding. My first bib shorts were wool. After a few hours, heavy with sweat, they stretched out, didn't stay in place, and ended up really hurting. Every time I stood up they slid down a few centimeters, threatening to hobble my knees and offend public decency – how true it is that, in order to be effective, bib shorts have to cling directly to the skin.

Nowadays bibs stay in place and, if you take the time to slather the insides with cream, you almost forget you have a butt.

As for the rest, things haven't evolved as much. There's a little foam pad in the palm of fingerless riding gloves. The shoes are rigid and shaped to facilitate pedaling, which is good; they're made of plastic, which isn't. Just about everybody now wears a helmet. Jerseys too are now made of synthetics, which isn't so brilliant. I wear bright colors, not to show off but to be seen by drivers. I have them in various colors, except yellow, which is a sacred color. You have to be a first-class dreamer to wear the yellow jersey. Only one of them exists, the one at the top of the pyramid, the one you go after on your bike. Any cyclist will tell you.

Nevertheless, I'm the happy owner of a yellow jersey, which I wear only in my room. It's the one given me by my friends of Oulipo after I won the Goncourt Prize for short stories at Saint-Quentin. That day I won a bike I can't use because it's not my size and a jersey I don't want to use because it's yellow. The two of them remain pristine treasures.

I have an old-style, pure wool jersey, purple with green borders, the colors of the 'Ace of Clubs' group of Saint-Étienne, the oldest bike-touring club in France. It's an honorary jersey I was given, and I cherish it. I cherish it so much that I don't wear it for fear of wearing it out, which isn't so smart.

They were faithful, those wool jerseys. They soaked up the sweat and dried on your back, and you felt like an old warrior when you came back from a ride, haloed with salt.

Shorts

One morning while I was riding in the Haute-Loire, I passed a cyclist going the other way. I greeted him with a little hand gesture, as 'serious' riders do ('serious' riders are those who recognize those riders worthy of a hand gesture; the others are just 'leeks' planted there), and it was then that I noticed on his black and red bib shorts the slogan 'Fournel, Packaging' [*Fournel, Emballage*]. I swung around, caught up with him, and announced that I wanted his shorts, since my name was written on them.

He was visibly astonished and unambiguously refused to part with them but agreed to give me the name of his club and coach, who agreed to give me the name of the club's president, whom I could contact. M. Fournel, manufacturer of packaging materials [*emballage*] in the plain of Forez, was happy to sell me some shorts bearing my name. Given that in cycling lingo 'to wrap it up' [*emballer*] means to sprint, you can imagine my pride.

So I wear shorts displaying my name and my ability – real or proclaimed – as a sprinter. Since I've never had occasion to sprint, nobody can verify it.

51

Biker's Tan

The ultimate outfit of the cyclist, the suit he wears when he's given up everything else, his tattoo, is his tan.

Conversely, the white part of my body looks like one of those old swimsuits. 'Getting a tan' terrifies me. The prospect of stretching out in the sun for ten minutes to roast myself utterly horrifies me.

It so happens that cycling is an outdoor sport often done in the sun. So you get a tan, even if you don't want it. The 'biker's tan' starts at the middle of the arm and descends to the glove. On the left side, it spares the watch. It starts halfway down the thigh and stops at the sock. It strikes the head and neck. If the same cyclist wears a cap, his white forehead sticks out, until now the mark of the Auvergnat peasant . . . None of this seems cool to the bare breast and string bikini crowd.

One summer Rémy and I rolled through the Alps from north to south: we went from Geneva to Saint-Tropez, doing all the great climbs along the way: the Izoard, the Vars, and the Allos on the next to the last day with the Verdon as dessert. We finished this little trip sated with the sun, fried and refried.

Arriving in Saint-Tropez in late afternoon, the first thing I had to do was swim in the Mediterranean. We caused a sensation. In the land of the tanning cult, these two big guys with their whitish bellies and swarthy limbs set off plenty of whispering and nudging. The babes practically died laughing.

I bear the marks of my biker's tan all winter. It's my second skin. I derive neither shame nor glory from it. I take it on, and, with the first rays of the spring sun, I put down another layer.

One day I was at the pool and a kid yelled at me: 'Hey pops, you forgot your bike!'

It's hard to stay incognito.

Legs

When I go out with someone for the first time I immediately glance at his legs to know how fast we're going to go and with what sauce I'm going to be eaten.

You can read a cyclist by his legs.

To see, early in the morning, before the start of the stage, the tanned and oiled forest of the *peloton*'s legs – that's something.

The bike lengthens muscles, makes them bigger around. The better the shape of the cyclist, the more defined the muscles. Freed of its fat, freed of its casing, the muscle is like an anatomy lesson.

To add to the spectacle, racers shave their legs, and their legs seem made of pure bronze.

If you come upon somebody who's shaved, beware: generally, they go fast, and they're in shape (the out-of-shape racer willingly lets his leg hair grow back). The slightly chubby leg, vaguely heavy and with indistinct contours, means, on the other hand, that there's still work to do, and that 'going for a ride' will be just that.

The slender leg, with a little bitty calf, belongs to the climber. The good-sized thigh – that's a sprinter. The long and harmonious leg – a *rouleur* (a racer on the flats). A short femur? He'll be swift. Rounded buttocks? He'll start strong. Slender ankles and knees mean class.

Contrary to what's usually claimed, fat calves aren't all that useful: the essential energy of the cyclist is concentrated in the back, the buttocks, and the thighs.

At the height of the season, it's difficult to forget one's legs. They are the site of curious physiological phenomena. The most surprising is 'big thighs.' With an accumulation of I don't know what kind of fatigue, the thighs swell up and get hard. They won't fit into your shorts, or your pants, and you find yourself burdened with two hams whose cycling worth is relative, at least for a few days.

When you're in shape, standing up can be painful. One of my friends was getting married, and I had to go to Mass – not a habit of mine. I found myself unable to stand, as do the faithful. I had the painful feeling that my legs wanted to move up into my trunk.

In that situation, only the bike can soothe the pain. After a few kilometers, it goes away – or it changes into cramps, for good.

I dream about massage. Just seeing the greediness with which racers 'go for a massage,' or their ill humor when their turn doesn't come, makes me think it must be a panacea. Masseurs occupy a special place: they are confidants, friends. Just by touching the muscles they know if it's been a hard day, if their racer is 'doing well' or is 'tight.' For a long time they had an obscure role and carried mysterious bags – like Coppi's blind masseur, who was supposed to have supplied him with all sorts of explosives.

I dream of a masseur who would supply me with supple muscles, unknotted cramps, and nice talk. That would give me two beautiful legs.

Double Bass

Throughout my childhood my extended family – cousins of both sexes – shared a wood and fiberboard house deep in a meadow in the Haute-Loire. It was jerry-built after the war for refugees. The refugees had left, and we rented it by the year. Everyone in the village knew it as 'The Shack,' which was perfectly appropriate.

Each family group had two identical rooms separated by thin wood sheeting; one of these rooms served as the kitchen–dining room, the other as the bedroom. After dark the two were transformed into garages: since we were afraid of robbers, rain, and the sneaky effect of dew on frames, we brought the bikes in. When all the bikes were inside, it became impossible to get out. The last one to go to bed brought in the last bike, and the first one up took them all out.

In life's orchestra, the bike is the double bass. Hard to forget it.

Transport

When he sets foot on earth, the cyclist looks like a vile duck and suddenly finds himself burdened with his beautiful bicycle. Nostalgia blurs his gaze – he was so close to flying, and here he is, a clumsy oaf.

I've tried everything, trying to transport my bicycle: boxes, bags, bike racks, baggage racks. My father even designed his own bike rack and had it made. It was so huge that people on the street thought it was a television antenna.

I've had every sort of accident. I lost a bike rack bristling with four bikes on the autoroute du Sud. I lost my beautiful blue bike on the autoroute de l'Ouest – a sharp dip in the road made it shoot off the trunk-mounted bike carrier, and I dragged it for a hundred meters. I held my mauve bike in my arms on an airplane, afraid that they would throw it in the hold like a common suitcase (I should mention that that one was made of super-thin, super-light steel – and that it broke not long afterward).

Nothing really works, and everything makes you want to do the whole trip on the bike. And you have to make sure that your inn really has a lockable and dry garage where your sled can snooze.

Still, the ideal actually exists, and I experienced it once. We were touring in the Swiss Alps, and at Saint-Moritz we stayed at a fancy hotel. When we arrived, the porter was stationed at the entry to the garage. He quickly relieved me of my bike, parked it among the Ferraris and Rolls-Royces, took off my saddlebag, and sent it up to my room.

Need for Air

Territory

My world as a child was always more vast than my village. As soon as I knew how to ride I grasped the idea of a greater world. When I left to do a circuit, everything inside the circuit was 'home.' In that way I traced ever larger circles as my strength developed – around Bas-en-Basset, and I appropriated Le Vert, Tiranges, Saint-Hilaire, Aurec, Yssingeaux, Malataverne, Retournac, Usson-en-Forez, Saint-Bonnet-le Château.

The Haute-Loire's mesh of roads is a blessing for the cyclist. They're narrow, serpentine, beautiful, and little traveled. The choice of routes is vast. The grades vary greatly and, though you always start at 425 meters and end up at 1,100, the profiles are always different: regular climbs, back breakers, switchbacks.

My village is lodged in the valley of the Loire, in a little flat area, and to get out you have to go up. Curiously, the six or seven climbs that let you out have very different landscapes: if the Tiranges climb is a beautiful ascent up the side of the valley that opens out as it approaches the summit, the Saint-Hilaire climb is shady, regular, deeply hidden, and smells of moss and mushrooms. The ascent via Thézenac is clear, hot, steep; its upper part opens onto the spectacle of the rounded volcanoes and plateaus of Velay.

In the distance, Mount Mézenc.

The villages and hamlets nod off and, even today, you can ride for three hours and meet only a couple of cars. The countryside is well maintained, and the little crooked fields alternate with peaceful pastures. The summer burns, the winter is rough, the seasons are well defined – it's an education in all roads and climates.

Little by little I enlarged my circles, on my father's wheel, faithfully; he sheltered me from the wind and silently taught me the cycling virtues.

There's something of the peasant in the pedaler. They share a taste for nature, submission to the elements, patience, thrift, obstinacy, and the sense of acceleration. There's something of the sprint in the harvest and the vintage. The eternal order of the fields converges with the eternal order of the road, and riders like Robic and Poulidor rode a bike the same way they worked the farm.

In that way, between the ages of nine and fifteen, I confidently covered hundreds of kilometers behind my father. I learned to climb and descend, I learned not to be afraid, to take advantage of everything, to be crazy at the right moment, not to be frightened of the Man with the Hammer. I changed bikes twice, I stretched out the seatpost and the stem, and, at fifteen, I went to the front.

It was the gentlest way of carrying out some Freudian ritual, with my father no doubt suffering from wounded cyclist's pride but comforted almost as much in his father's, and route guide's, pride. I was jubilant.

He soon called me 'the beast of burden' because of the energy – perhaps nuanceless – that I put into pedaling, and the nickname stuck.

And then it was on the same roads that I learned the virtues of battle and shoot-'em-ups with Furnon, Madel, and the local lead-foots. It was no longer a question of patience: my mouth was hanging open and my quads were on fire. Now only the results counted.

Flats

The only thing my routes of the Haute-Loire concealed from me was the flats.

When, on turning twenty, I 'went up' to Paris for the right reasons, I discovered the flats. And I was amazed when I understood that I had to learn.

I thought the flats were a kind of boring Eden, a gift to geezer riders. I was wrong. The flats entail a particular cycling science. My biggest surprise was the change in length: on my little routes I had to push hard, but every intense half-hour was rewarded with ten minutes of rest.

Changes in activity level and position were very frequent. On the flats, it's not the same deal; you can spend five or six hours without stopping pedaling, without changing position, and new pains start to appear: weariness, for example, shoulder difficulties, a sore neck.

My use of the derailleur up to that point was fairly radical: from 42 x 22 I'd jump to 52 x 14. On the flats, I had to learn the merits of going from tooth to tooth. There can be a chasm between 53 x 16 and 53 x 17, and as a general rule it's the wind that carves it out.

The Haute-Loire isn't spared winds, but they're blocked by mountains and get entangled in rises, forests, ridges. They surprise you in sudden ambushes and then disappear. On the plains they lead the dance, and their presence is continuous.

Bike position becomes crucial, and shelter becomes a science. One finds oneself constantly trying to determine the direction of the breeze to find a bit of shelter on a friendly wheel.

On the Vauhallan plateau the wind blowing from the west fans out the Sunday riders, and trying to start out against it is a challenge pretty much equivalent to attacking a hill.

The reward of the flats – for there is one – is the fantastic group output you can attain. On days of grace, with four or five of equal strength and strong will, you can cover considerable terrain at extraordinary speed. The musketeer style ('one for all and all for one') is the most voluptuous way of managing the flats.

By Heart

I know my area of the Haute-Loire by heart.

Knowing means having reference points, being able to figure out where you are, calibrating yourself.

My standard measure is a climb of barely ten kilometers that comes out of the valley of the Ance and leads up to the village of Tiranges. It's a splendid route, a ledge on the side of a mountain, under shady pines, with slightly tangier smells than those of Provence. A country road, two cars wide, and a rough surface. A road crossed by lizards and snakes, with brambles, ferns, and blondish rocks on the sides. A road that feels like a path as it goes up; it was laid out more by the steps of people and animals than by the will of bulldozers. It has short level stretches and serious leg-breakers. It's charming.

I especially like it because, before going up, it meanders in the valley for five kilometers and gives you time to warm up. The river sends out a last little bit of coolness and, after the little bridge on the left, and after the old abandoned bistro where the organ grinder used to play, things start to get serious.

By the first hundred meters, I know if I'm a 39 x 24 or a 39 x 20 – in other words, whether I'm sort of in shape or in good shape (these mystical numbers indicate gearing; the first is significantly lower than the second). After that, I don't even have to look at my watch anymore – just the pace of the landscape going by and the sequence of my sensations are enough to tell me where I am.

I recognize the two turns where I have to stand on the pedals, the little ledge that will seem long, and the hamlet where I'll start to feel it in my legs, generally when I get to the watering hole. If I have to accelerate, it'll be on leaving the forest because accelerating there is really hard on the legs (and not just on mine).

And then, on the other side of the hamlet called Chasles, I know there will be a level stretch amid the rye. The view will open up. We'll catch sight of the rounded crests of the Velay. The kestrels will be turning above our heads, the chickens will be pecking on the side of the road, and we'll feel the slight breeze coming from Saint-Pal. It will be time to take a drink and get ready for the last rise on the slope taking us through the hamlet of Les Arnauds. After that we will have to choose between the little road on the plateau that leads us to the switchbacks of Cacharrat and the Tiranges road that plunges back into the valley, passing above the medieval chateau of Saint-André-de-Chalançon, perched on its peak.

All this is ticked off in internal minutes that tell you whether it's May or July, whether you're rundown or in shape.

Cyclists are very familiar with this secret connection to the world. They have a nice expression for it: 'You're starting to feel it.'

69

The Ideal Vacation

My ideal vacation starts at the beginning of July. Work in Paris is slowing down. The last cocktails have been served. Summer books have been out for a number of weeks, the fall books are at the printer, and the Tour de France is still in the first, flat stages. The need for silence has become crucial. It's time to get on the road.

A little handlebar bag with the absolute minimum, and the road heading south. To travel to the Haute-Loire, near Saint-Étienne, as I do every summer, I take a series of secondary roads that lead me to the Loire and cross it at Orléans or Giens, follow the river on its left bank, and then continue along the accompanying canal at Allier, reaching Moulins, then Courpière, then Vichy; it gets serious in the Forez mountains: Job, Vertolaye, Ambert, Saint-Anthème, Usson, Saint-Hilaire-Cusson-la-Valmite, and Bas-en-Basset.

Four days of perfect peace without saying anything other than what's dictated by the bike's refrains, four days of hard-core silence to purge me of the torrent of words that constitute my everyday work, four days of physical violence to get revenge on my armchair. There's nobody on these French back roads and the transformation of *Homo intellectus* into *Homo bicycletus* takes place in private.

First, still in my Parisian muddle, I start to establish contact with my legs, in order to patch things up. Depending on the time of day, the old dramas come back: a former disagreement with my knee, an old crease on the saddle, a tight shoulder. But the old feeling of wellness also returns: a lightness of the thigh, a swelling of the calf, power coming from my back. From the need for silence, I slip into the need for rhythm.

Old secrets and new discoveries come together while my body, hot and active, seeks equilibrium with the outside. Weather stops being an abstraction, and the rain front that's passing through from west to east suddenly starts squishing in my shoes. It could also be the strong mistral wind that takes me by the shoulders and pushes me south with the speed of a CGV (*cycliste à grande vitesse*).

I cover 150 to 200 kilometers a day, and, if I can maintain a regular pace (at least so long as the road is flat), my mood changes and definitely lightens up as the trip progresses. I no longer torture myself with questions; I'm alive and soaked.

Toward the end of the afternoon, when I'm starting to feel the weight of the luggage, I look for a TV in a bistro, to watch the end of the Tour stage.

The riders are on the flats, the stakes are minimal, but the spectacle of the teams' larger maneuverings interests me. As a general rule all this makes for boring TV, but when your thighs have been educated a bit the spectacle of a team working flat out over the last twenty Ks to put its sprinter in orbit turns into an enjoyable tidbit. This is when you see the anonymous and proud locomotives. After that, it's up to the sprinter to sprint. He can be dangerous (Abdu-japarov), powerful (Ludwig), or simply magnificent (Cipollini, *il magnifico*).

The bike gives a new flavor to simple things: the shower, the bath, the bed you stretch out on, the smell of the cream you put on your legs – magic cream you put on out of gratitude, out of desire for a closer connection with your own body.

After I've pulled into port, the remaining ten days of vacation play themselves out following an immutable rhythm: bike in the morning, Tour de France in the afternoon. I can speak again; I'm a cyclist who talks, and I can pedal with friends: the biking friends who are still where I left them last year, around the fountain at seven in the morning (Jean-Loup, Titch); friends passing through with whom I ride elsewhere (Jean-Noël, Rémy, Sébastien); new people, strangers, riders.

About when it gets hot I like to watch the day's stage with my father. He's the guardian of the history and legends of the Tour, the commentator on the commentaries. Then, when the stage is over, and the sun is still well above the horizon of the Haute-Loire, it's time to move on to all the trivial vacation activities.

Around July 20, on a nice Sunday afternoon, the racers suddenly show up on the Champs-Elysées, and the Tour de France is over. My vacation finishes along with it in a big letdown, which I'll purge on my bike Monday morning, by myself in the green mountains and the scent of pines. My summer's over.

After that, I 'go back up' to Paris, with my bike on the roof of the car – it's true that, when I'm not going in circles, my cycling tropism heads south. Even if it's much easier to go from the Haute-Loire to Paris, even if the road descends at a steady rate for the first two hundred kilometers, going to Paris is 'going up.' My schoolteachers and the Michelin Man orient their maps that way, and in the same way they've oriented my destiny as a cyclist.

As a professional, I would have won Paris-Nice.

Giono

It was the middle of August and rather than staying near the Mediterranean shore, caressed by wind and spoiled by water, we took off to ride in the sun-bleached backcountry. On the afternoon of the second day, we were crossing the great deserted plain of Canjuers, where you occasionally come upon a tank. It's a deserted plateau under which, they say, huge weapons are stirring. In vain one looks for a tree, a shadow.

During the ride my father was telling me about the Provençal novelist Jean Giono, about the peasants of Provence and the way they welcome people, when I became unbearably thirsty – still, it was my father who was talking, not me. My water bottle was empty, his was too, and my little physique – I couldn't have been more than twelve or thirteen – was threatening collapse. My kisser must have been red enough to convince my father to take the dirt road, on the left, and to knock on the door of the only farmhouse in the area and ask for water. The farmer's wife opened the door a crack, stuck out her olive-colored face and black hair, and quite simply refused to give me anything to drink.

That's how I first crashed into Giono's world.

Around the Tour

We often set out to see the Tour de France. My father's idea was to get together some cousins, some friends, boys and girls, and organize a *grupetto* to go and pay homage to the racers at the top of the alpine passes.

Paying homage to the racers means first climbing the passes on bikes, ahead of them. We made sure we had one or two drivers who weren't turned off by the spectacle of cycling, or by driving slowly, and then we drew up our route.

It's pure pleasure to go up the passes in the morning, before the racers. The road is closed to cars, and going up a pass under these conditions is a real gift.

If you like solitude, go up the side the racers will come down. One summer I did this with Rémy; we linked up the Izoard, Vars, and Allais, riding against the course. Those three climbs are still a dazzling memory. You just have to get up early.

If you like crowds, follow the route of the racers. This way you feel what the crowd contributes to the race. You also get the spectacle of the endless picnic that is the Tour de France, and it's a way to pick up some firsthand info on the fans.

There are the hardworking types who write Richard Virenque's name in white paint on the road, and who yell at you if you ride over their fresh daubs. There are the picnickers with red faces who make up for going up on foot by attacking their first lunch. There are the pushers who want to help you with strong hands on your butt (when my wife is along she always gets more help than I do). And there are the noisemakers who practice their war chants on the riders passing through.

Occasionally you pick up a few wonderful pearls. I remember a big strong guy who ran a few meters behind my wife yelling, 'Go, Momerckx!'

You go up like this almost until the announcement of the break-away. At that point you sit down on the side and wait for the race, like a bike racer on foot.

Flags

I've gone up unbelievable passes but gotten no credit for it because a champion hadn't marked them.

Back from vacation, if I say to a friend: 'I climbed the Finestre pass,' he might reply: 'Well, I took it easy in the Caribbean.' On the other hand, if I tell him: 'Hey, I went up the Izoard,' his face lights up.

It's the same if I mention the Puy de Dôme, Alpe-d'Huez, Tourmalet, Vars, or Pra-Loup.

Whether they know it or not, whether they want it or not, the French have had an excellent cycling education. They know the champions and the locales of their exploits. The great champions superimpose their own geography on official geography. They're like little flags stuck on the map, or landmarks.

You can even tell the age and orientation of the person you're talking to. If his face lights up on hearing 'Pra-Loup,' he's a Théveno-Merckxian; 'Puy de Dôme,' he's an Anquetilo-Poulidorian; and if it's 'Alpe-d'Huez,' he's an Induraino-Züllian.

Maps

The day before a ride, or even that morning, my father had me read the map. We stood beside each other at the table, and I followed with my finger. That's how I learned the secret of yellow roads, white roads, and dangerous stretches marked with red dashes.

We left the main roads to the cars and sketched out our routes on everything else.

I especially watched out for the little arrows ('hooks,' my father, who knew the lingo, called them). On the maps in those days they scrupulously indicated the climbs: one hook for modest inclines, two for serious ascents, three for walls.

Those were still the days when cars got out of breath on the steep stretches, and stopped, with foam on their lips, to catch their breath and drink some water – human cars.

I also learned to count the kilometers by mentally adding all the little numbers that marked the route.

We did our ride and, after getting back, we reread the map to check the detours inspiration had led us on, and to assure ourselves that we really had done *that*. That's how I learned to tell north from south. I rarely get lost.

Road maps for me are dream machines. I like to read them as if they're adventure stories. When I drive my car I use them to find the shortest route, to find the long roads where cities join, roads that don't go through the country. As a bike rider I use them for everything else. If I know an area, every centimeter of the map is a landscape laid out before me. If I don't know it yet, every centimeter is an imagined landscape that I will explore. For example, I like maps of Brittany, which is a cyclist's region I've never ridden. It's my storeroom, my wine cellar. It's the masterpiece in my library I've not yet read.

Wind

The bike is the school of the wind.

There are two kinds of biking wind: objective wind and relative wind. The first one is produced by the world around us, and the second is the work of the cyclist alone. His masterpiece, you might say, for the faster he is, the more wind he creates.

The wind of the world is the one that hits you square on. Against it there's no remedy other than friendship and solidarity. When you get a strong, persistent north wind full in the face, there's nothing better than a big-shouldered friend. You curl up into a little ball behind him and wait for it to pass. Actually, you wait till he moves aside to give you his spot, and then you take your pull.

The strongest wind I can recall ever having ridden into is the wind of the west of Ireland. I pedaled along the coast, south of Galway, and I was careful always to leave riding into the wind, so I could be sure of getting back. I was alone, and it was a rough fight. There was no mercy. Everything that allows you to cheat and find shelter was missing: no trees, no houses, no hedges, no contours. Nothing but the wet, powerful, inexhaustible ocean wind. Stretched out on the bike, I had the feeling I was killing time, condemned to using mountain gears on flat terrain.

On the way back, all along the Irish coast, it was sheer delight when my little inner breath connected with the big outside wind. More pleasurable than descending, because I felt like I was in super shape, going much faster than I should have been.

Having very early on, at my own expense, learned that the wind wears you out, I soon learned to note from which direction it was blowing. There's something of the sailor in the cyclist. Thanks to this basic training you learn to shelter yourself better and take better advantage of the strength of others. When the wind blows from the side, or from an angle, the riders fan out across the road in order to use their companions as barriers. These fans are called 'echelons,' and if you're not in the right one, getting from one to another is practically impossible.

The relative wind made by the cyclist is that of his own speed. You can feel it when a rider brushes against you. You can also feel it when a faster cyclist passes you – they call it 'catching cold.'

One day going up the Pilat and not dawdling, I 'caught a cold' in this way from a young lady as agile as a gazelle, who was climbing like an airplane. Did she ever have a nice pedal stroke! It was a real pleasure to see her, locked in her rhythm, dusting me off with a bit of breeze.

Luckily for me I was able to get on her wheel. The cyclist, by creating a wind, hollows out a space in which it's easy to ride. If you stay locked onto the rear wheel you'll do 25 percent less work. Merci, gazelle.

Shelter and suction are the best reasons to make cycling friends. You can benefit from the combined effort and relax for a moment before taking your turn at the front.

To really take advantage, you have to stay close, in the bubble, with your front wheel only a few centimeters from the wheel in front.

If you give up a few bike-lengths, the wind closes in on you and 'getting back in' is not easy. When whoever's in front is pulling really hard, it can even be impossible.

In the 1996 Tour de France, in the long and very regular descent from Montgenèvre to Briançon, the *peloton*, anxious to get to the finish, stretched out in a long unbroken line, with every racer fighting to keep his place. Melchor Mauri, a good-looking rider who had been pedaling next to our car, had some derailleur problems that made him lose his spot; he was slipping away very quickly from the group. Christian Palka, who was driving, told me: 'If we leave him there, he'll soon be ten minutes down. He won't get back in by himself at that speed.'

So we sheltered him with our car for about a hundred meters, to get him back in the line. He thanked us with a pleasant wink. At that point we were doing about eighty kilometers an hour.

Please don't repeat this story, since it's strictly forbidden by race rules to help riders in this way – by breaking the terrible law of the wind.

Sounds

The sound of bikes is the sound of the wind. The machine itself should be almost silent.

In the old days bikes leaked dirty oil and grease; today they're more discreet, but the lubrication is no less effective. A real bike does not squeak, rub, groan; it purrs. In flat country, you shouldn't hear it. If by chance you pass a wall, you can make out the light hum of the chain on the cog. On the other hand it's much easier to hear other people's bikes, especially the slight clicking sound of someone changing gears, which tells you you'll have to change your pace.

Indexed derailleurs nowadays save us from the irritating grinding of the chain when it's stuck between cogs.

Sew-ups have their own whistling sound, especially when you stand up to accelerate. Now that clinchers are in general use, this whistling can go into the Sound Museum. It'll be on display there along with the tinkling of the bell, the creaking of the leather saddle, and the rubbing of the fender on the tire.

Brakes have quieted down as well. The more efficient rubber of the brake shoes now does its job gently, silently.

The *peloton*, on the other hand, makes noise.

From the outside, it's a powerful and low-pitched breathing, a breathing that no mechanical noise could conceal. If it were a locomotive it would be a high-speed TGV rather than a steam engine.

From the inside, the sound comes from a hundred little noises that all add up. A hundred derailleurs, a hundred chains, a hundred gear changes at once, all of that locked in a mobile cocoon in which sounds pass from front to back.

If you're adroit enough to maintain your position, the *peloton* is a protective bubble that isolates you and pulls you forward.

If you listen closely, you can make out bits of chatter, laughter, quick commands. At the start of a climb it's fun – but when you really start to gasp and fight for air, and you hear somebody who's still cracking jokes, it's not as amusing.

For about ten years now, since toe-clips disappeared, the *peloton* makes a new sound. I became aware of it one morning around seven o'clock in downtown Saint-Étienne. There were about a thousand of us at the start of a hill climb and, at the pistol shot of the starter, we clicked into our two thousand clipless pedals.

In the Sunday morning silence it was a good sound, and it said: 'Time to get going.'

Descending

Descending reassembles me. The descent reunites the skier and cyclist in me. Every descent on a bike is like a giant slalom, with its tricky spots, its braking spots, and its indispensable sense of anticipation.

To descend well, you've got to have an excellent knowledge of the road – a kind of complicity with the engineers who built it, an instinctive and rapid grasp of the terrain. Every road is a design, and every descent is a design within the design.

Modern roads dictate their law to the terrain with crashing bulldozers and dynamite explosions, but the old ones embrace the contours of earth and mountain.

When you go into a blind turn, it's essential to have an intuitive idea of what comes next – so experience is essential. The more you descend, the faster you descend.

You must be watchful and fit. Descending is the opposite of letting yourself go. That's why I admire so much the racers who, after a terrible battle on the climb, pitch themselves full-tilt down the other side.

The great descenders are strange creatures whom you have to learn to be on guard against. I've followed a few down. They're not necessarily mean, but their virtuosity can transform them. Everything makes it seem as if they want to put their adversaries to sleep. They go to the front, make you feel confident; then it's suddenly bang, and you're down, in the ditch, in the ravine. A few people can turn where everyone else goes straight. This is good to know.

The pleasure of doing a descent you've already done a thousand times lies in braking as little as possible, holding back on the brakes, entering the turns as fast as possible, coming out with a good line to attack the next turn, tracing out an impeccable design, and giving it the rhythm of music. You can sing going down.

You can do this at medium speed and enjoy it a lot.

If on the other hand you're tired, or just feeling dull, a descent down a pass can seem endless. If it's cold and your fingers are numb, if it's raining and your brakes don't work, if the wind is blasting across the road, descending can be torture.

I remember a descent from the Ventoux into a cold mistral wind that left me frozen stiff in Malaucène, unable to thaw, and, even worse, unable to recall any of the pleasures of the climb.

Smells

Biking smells good.

In the Haute-Loire, it smells of pine and moss, with touches of new-mown hay. Here and there, a spot of cow.

Sometimes in hamlets a cowshed makes its presence known. But also the smell of open windows: beef stew, wax, detergent, roast chicken. Thrown over a line, sheets and blankets emit a night odor, quickly lost in the blue of the sky.

The summer itself has a very strong smell. You pass through pockets of sweet-smelling heat, when the road cuts through a wheat or rye field, where you come out of a forest and enter a clearing. The heat activates the smell of the resins, and brings up out of the road the smell of tar, the profound background to all the summer scents.

A great concert takes place just after a rain, when the road surface is still steaming from the storm and the deep odors of the world ascend from the earth. The sun, just back, dries your jersey and draws out of your own body the aroma of wool and salt. The smell of water gradually dissipates and for a quarter of an hour you feel as if you're riding inside a truffle.

For a long time these were the smells of biking for me. When you ride fast and lose your breath, they merge and swirl in an ever-changing rainbow.

Since I've expanded my cycling domain, my range has grown to include the smell of fish, sand, and flowers in California; the smell of the wood fires of chalets in Austria; the smell of lavender and thyme in Provence; the smell of salt in Ireland; the smell of the great damp autumn undergrowth of Paris; and the fine, fresh, pure smell of the high mountains.

Landscapes

Contrary to what happens when I'm in a car and the landscape allows itself to be seen and not 'be,' on a bike I'm sitting in it.

With the bike there's an animal relation with the world: the mountains you see are there to be scaled, the valleys are for cruising down into, shadows are for hiding in and stretching out. To be in the landscape, in its heat, its rain, its wind, is to see it with different eyes; it's to impregnate oneself with it in an instinctive and profound way. The mountain rising before me isn't a mountain, it's first a grade to climb, a test, a doubt, sometimes anxiety. At the summit, it's a conquest, lightness. I've taken it and it's in me.

In some ways the beautiful stretch in the forest of the Izoard belongs to me, the road on the side of the Aubisque belongs to me, the gorges of the Tarn and the Verdon belong to me, and the Rambouillet forest too. I've sweated them. They've never been a spectacle; we've played together.

*　*　*

When I set out in the morning I'm still in a homebody mood, still in a warm-bed mood. I'm cold; my cyclist's micro-pains revive. My right knee balks, there's a fleeting pain down by the saddle, my back's stiff. The road is gray and vaguely hostile. I grind away at a sullen low gear. I have the impression that my legs are hard and the universe is soft. I don't see anything.

After a few kilometers my temperature rises, I no longer feel bad, and the world unfolds around me. I enter the landscape, gently. Equilibrium is established, relating to the heat, the rain, the wind. If I'm in shape this equilibrium will be maintained, even if the conditions change. The sharp coolness at the top of the hill will be a blessing, as will the warmth suddenly encountered when I redescend into the valley.

What I see of the world embellishes what I feel of it and me. On the little tiny road leading from Thézenac to Cacharrat, there's a brief stretch of a hundred meters that's protected by trees, a stretch that no doubt hides a spring, and that preserves, even on the hottest days, a breath of cool air. Thanks to this 'cool spot,' which I pass through in a few seconds and where I don't think I've ever actually stopped, I can ride for two or three hours for the sole pleasure of rediscovering it and feeling on my skin, for an instant, that old sensation, as old as my childhood, just like the day I first experienced it with a smile of well-being and relief.

When I ride in faraway places in unknown climes, I have to tame them before being able to discover, for good, the surrounding world.

When I arrived in California, where nature is chronically enchanting, I first had to learn to ride in what for me was an unknown mix of burning sun and freezing wind, going from winter to summer – depending on whether I was in shade or sun – and invited to dress and undress twenty times a day. Only then could I feast on the sequoias and the golden prairies, the gray and roiling Pacific that watches you pass with a frown, the thousands of flowers planted by the wind on the edge of the road.

I also have my bestiary. If my observations are correct, there are two great categories of animals: those who'd like to ride a bike, and those who love to watch the spectacle of cyclists.

Cows, who were thought to specialize in trains, like to feast their eyes on cyclists as well. Whether in Normandy, the Bourbonnais, or the Forez, they follow you lazily with their gaze, with their gentle air.

In the Haute-Loire, hawks too are up for the spectacle. They fly in distant circles above your helmet.

I very much liked the climb up the Vars pass on the north side. It was a consistent climb, the way up pleasant in its succession of small villages. Perhaps it was among my favorites. Today the road has been widened for buses, and the mountain is scarred over with ski lifts – 'yet another one fucked,' Queneau would have said. One morning while I was climbing it alone and in silence I met, on the short flat stretch at the top, my most attentive and unexpected spectator: a marmot. This ordinarily secretive and timid guy was waiting for me, sitting on his rump, his forepaws resting on his chest, and his eyes sharp. I stopped, put my bike on the ground, and we stood there facing each other, ten meters apart. When he was satisfied with his inspection, having sufficiently sniffed and observed me, he left to store my image for the winter.

Among all the animals who would like to ride a bike, no doubt dogs are the most irresponsible. Envious, they snap at your calves, and playful, they frisk about in front of your front wheel – when they don't do worse. Horses will offer a bit of trotting on the path beside the road, happy to have the opportunity to gun it.

On the tiny road that goes from Beauzac to Sarlanges, below the Frétisse, I had as a fellow traveler a big, wonderful, nice hare. We did a hundred meters together. He stayed on my right, near the ditch, and galloped. I was fascinated by the sight of his ears flopping to the tempo, and by the sound of his running on the sand and asphalt. He wasn't scared – not even wary. He was following his route, which was my route, and then he went back into the brush, which was his brush.

I experienced them in Ireland and rediscovered them in California, on my treks along the Pacific coast: seagulls. They're the worst. When they get bored, they set their sights on you and dive. Their motives are strange; they don't intend to eat you, or to steal your bike, but you'd swear they're aggressively, secretly, suspiciously plotting. When I rode through Bodega Bay – the very place Hitchcock filmed *The Birds* – I reacted to their swooping on me with a not at all vague disquiet. They take aim from afar, as soon as they see you; then they pass right over your head, screaming, with a great fluttering of wings. They can do that ten times. Three or four of them will join in, until you've gone on your way. They've managed to scare me.

In France, the landscape changes quickly, and the speed of the bike allows you to sample all the variations. In the same day you can change 'regions' three or four times, and the succession of landscapes is extremely appealing. Our country is cyclable thanks to its tight network of roads and variety of landforms. You can go gently, slipping from the Loire region to the soft plumpness of the Bourbonnais to the ancient heights of the Morvan. You can also make radical transitions: take the road south from Pau and ride straight into the barrier of the Pyrénées, or leave Lourdes and climb up to Hautacam as if scaling a wall.

The bike's speed makes one be selective as to the surrounding landscape. Your eyes have to go right to the essential and keep alert if they want to grasp an anecdote, a bit of passing beauty, some fleeting charm.

Why, in the immense landscape of the Vars, did I see only the marmot? Why did my eye know that he was waiting for me there?

In the Year 2000

New Year's 2000 was a commercial flop. The idea of the business people was to turn the world upside down, sending everyone to the ends of the earth with a pointy hat, a noisemaker, and a bottle of champagne. In San Francisco they were waiting for Parisian Society. The part that hadn't gone to Auckland anyway.

The inhabitants of Earth chose instead to stay home and celebrate in other ways. Which allows one to be optimistic concerning the next millennium celebration. San Francisco was, therefore, calm on the night of December 31, even a little gloomy, since the shopkeepers had boarded up their windows out of fear of the Parisians.

I didn't suspect this a week before, so I treated myself to a cycling celebration in the desert, far from the expected tumult. The idea was to cross Death Valley on a bike.

After a night in Lone Pine, where John Wayne and Gary Cooper stayed when making westerns, after a breakfast on the wooden porch of a ranch located at the valley's entrance, facing a sun rising on maximum Nothingness, my son and I hit the road (my son isn't a cyclist, but he rides a bike very well).

Death Valley's appeal is that it offers all the desert forms: dunes, rocks, salt lakes, color palettes. The value of crossing it on January 1 is that the sun stays low on the horizon and brings out the entire range of colors, without overwhelming anything. And the heat is bearable.

I wanted to start from the lowest point of the valley, about three hundred meters below sea level, to climb to the summit of Dante's Peak, around seventeen hundred meters higher, and see the panorama of the entire valley. The way up is beautiful, steady, with long straight lines and a terrible final kilometer. The grade is comparable to that of a major alpine pass. Traffic is nonexistent, and it's strongly recommended that you bring water bottles and a hot-water bottle if you're planning on staying outside after night falls.

The spectacle is exceptional, grand, sublime, etc., but it's not cycling-related. As for a lot of American landscapes, the bike's rhythm is just not appropriate. Either the bike doesn't go fast enough or the landscape doesn't change quickly enough, but something resists the marriage. This sort of landscape is made to measure for the car. Lost in these immense straight lines, I felt like a displaced animal, a Sempé cartoon character who's too small for his surroundings, a minuscule trace of life in Death Valley.

I experienced something new there. The air was so dry that I had the feeling it was sucking up my sweat. As soon as a droplet formed on my forehead it evaporated, was absorbed, vanished into the clear blue sky. Sweat is a carapace, it's armor, surrounding and protecting you from contact with the world. To work up a sweat is to pull on the matador's garb. There I was, naked; I climbed with a quick rhythm because the road was good and the day was short, but in spite of everything I had the feeling that my carburetor wasn't working properly. I tried to get it right for the whole climb and reached the top without having achieved it.

At the top I got my reward. The World was magical and beautiful, as old as it is, quiet like nowhere else, indifferent to the little hiccup of the millennium. I waited for day's end and the frigid cold of the night. The millions of stars.

There we were in the year 2000, and my first resolution was to redo this ride at the beginning of each century, to check my fitness.

Ventoux

There are plenty of passes higher than the Ventoux. Every cyclist knows the sacred monsters with their holy of holies and their land-scapes: the tunnel of the Galibier; the lonely wasteland of the Izoard; the last two stifling kilometers of the Restefonds; the switchbacks of the Alpe-d'Huez; the badly packed earth of the Gavia; or the terrible right turn of the Saint-Charles bridge in the Iseran . . . So many legendary places where cyclists head, like pilgrims.

The Ventoux is alone. Sitting on a plain. It overlooks no valley, it leads nowhere. Its only purpose is to be climbed.

It is its own climate and country. It has its own specific fauna, processionary caterpillars and beetles, and its flora, villous Greenland poppies and Spitzberg saxifrage. It defies the wind, and on days of heavenly grace, it offers up an immense panorama.

It's an enigma to the cyclist.

You never climb the same Ventoux twice. Every cyclist has a mem-ory of a glorious ascent. The one I did with my sister one delightful morning, in Provençal harmony and the north wind. The one Jean-Noël Blanc did on the closed road, between two walls of snow, in a Ventoux his alone.

In the same way, everyone can remember leaden days when, suddenly, for no reason, the bike freezes, blocked on the asphalt. Those days of cold sweat, days when the fruit rots in your pockets and when, very quickly, a dull anguish seizes your heart.

On one of those ugly days I had used up my water reserves halfway up the north side. It was blazing hot, the heat of a stormy August 15. I noticed a water spout on the side of the road and ran over to fill my water bottles. The dripping faucet was unapproachable, black with a swarming cluster of wasps and insects.

It was only ten in the morning. Already the tar was melting, and my bottles stayed empty.

There are no more landmarks in these nightmare climbs. Your eyes stay glued on your front wheel, and it's your innards you're staring at there, without really seeing them. The friend who was climbing so slowly down below passes you. In slow motion you cut a mule trail in the straight grain of the road. Cars honk their horns. You don't even think about going back down. You're not thinking about anything any more.

The Ventoux has no in-itself. It's the greatest revelation of your-self. It simply feeds back your fatigue and fear. It has total knowledge of the shape you're in, your capacity for cycling happiness, and for happiness in general. It's yourself you're climbing. If you don't want to know, stay at the bottom.

Pedaling Within

Velodrome

It was made completely of wood, like an old scow, and it creaked in every joint. It was full of smoke and dust, full of cigarette butts. You sat on bleachers among tough guys who yelled above the brouhaha. I was very small, and I made myself even smaller, lost in terrorized jubilation just to be in the Vel d'Hiv.

Saint-Étienne was one of the rare cities to have one, but it was so dilapidated and so dangerous they tore it down. My adolescent years passed to the rhythm of the progressive forgetting of the promise to build another one. Now nobody even thinks about it.

I'm a fan of the 'squirrels.' They're the virtuosic froth of cycling. I see them as a little crazy, a little autistic, their eyes trained on the wheel in front of them, focused on their effort, locked into their virtuosity, powerful and feline, pulled forward by their fixed gear (they can't stop pedaling), without brakes, having chosen to be what the bicycle most radically is: pure speed.

Track racing is the essence of the bicycle, of cycling interiority, of the opposite. Bikes with pure lines, stripped of everything, simple and intense rules, a changing and intoxicating spectacle, a fundamental sadness among racers deprived of air and countryside, day and night. A mysterious spectacle that used to be to everyone's taste, and which now nobody likes, without one's being able to tell which died first – the supply or the demand.

André Pousse liked to recount his old trackie memories, his memories of the Six Day races, his disgust with road racing, his ruses, his scheming, his sinister hunt-downs at two in the morning, and the little subtle tug at the neck you feel every time you come into a turn almost horizontally, and which, as the hours pass, makes your neck and shoulders heavy as stone . . .

I high-tailed it over to Bercy when they tried to revive the old magic there. There really was a track; there really were famous racers . . . and not much else. The ambiance of the velodrome was gone.

In the Saint-Étienne velodrome I saw Coppi, old; I saw Anquetil; I saw Rivière – battling it out together. I saw the crazy paced riders behind their motorbikes, which added a whiff of gasoline to the tobacco smoke – at the end of the events you had the impression they were pedaling around inside a pipe. I saw the relay racers launched with a push on their shorts; the Madison specialists, so numerous on the track that you ended up seeing only the wildness; the pure sprinters, poised at the top of their vertiginous turns, lords of the realm.

I liked to station myself at the top of a turn, exactly at the spot where the grade is steepest, where the sprinters like to come and mark time before plunging back down to the baseline and surprising their adversary.

I dreamed of relishing that feeling, me, the chubby kid sitting up there in the box next to Roger Rivière's actual mother, who was looking lovingly at her son.

I've retained such a vivid memory of a few of those evenings, spent there with my father, that the desire to ride on the track has never left me. And I never have done it – since there was no track.

I did experience an ersatz version of it, when, much later on, I had the chance to ride a bike on the auto circuit at Monthléry. The pitch was there, and, with it, the worry about going fast enough so as not to scrape the ground with the outside pedal, but everything else was missing: the wood, the grave and whistling sound of silk tires, the tight angles at the corners, the asphyxiating atmosphere. The velodrome.

The Texture of the Roads

Suddenly the road gets smoother, my legs turn more freely. Automatically I shift into a higher gear, move back on the saddle. I've just changed *départements*, changed texture.

Every *département*, sometimes every district, has its own way of tarring back roads; each has its own idea of ideal asphalt, of perfect paving. For the cyclist, this is translated by a little bump when a boundary is crossed, and by a new feel in the ride.

In the mountains, where the winter cold bites into the tar, and the summer heat resoftens it, the road's texture is rough and dark: a Beluga that livens you up with tiny vibrations, stiffening your perineum and, little by little, making your hands tingle through the gloves. In the descent the roughness comes up on both sides of your spine, as far as your shoulders, where it vibrates to the same rhythm as your arms and palms.

On the climb, on really hard days, every bit of gravel is a minuscule mountain you climb in addition to the mountain itself – it's then that they say the road is 'paying back' badly, which clearly means that you have to give more.

When in spring I get back on my familiar roads, I find the frost has bitten into the surface; it's crazed. Over winter the trucks have opened potholes. The repair crews have patched them with black gunk they smooth over with the back of a shovel. Generous guys make a mound, stingy ones leave a hole. In both cases I bounce around and my tires pick up gravel bits. If I don't swipe them off with my glove they bump every 2.198 meters, and I risk a flat. Heat and cold, along with hundreds of cars going over them, are needed for these dark patches to merge into the overall asphalt, leaving a stain that stretches out over the years. On these rough-textured roads, spring rains trace out streaks of red earth, storms scatter broken branches, and autumn dumps wet leaves.

In the ditches nettles and brambles shoot up, calf high. If the road crew is late, green grass sprouts right in the middle of the road, through the broken crust.

When I return, the road in the valley is fine-grained. It's light in color and follows a canal, as smooth as calm water. My breathing is easier, and if I step on it, the road 'pays back' well.

By dint of riding little back roads, long distance trips, loops around my village, I've built up saddle memory.

From the packed dirt of the old Dolomite passes to the smooth cement of the autoroutes (I've been able to ride them before their official opening to car traffic), via the beautiful coatings that make you feel as if you're on rubber, and the cobbles, and the roads laid down in slabs that go 'plock plock' at the expansion joints, I could write a catalog of all the sensations I've registered.

The cyclist's derrière is the locus of historic dramas, of furious boils, of sneaky swellings that alter the outcome of races. For me it's the locus of a particular intelligible sensitivity. With my eyes closed I'm sure I could recognize, just by sitting in the saddle, the texture that a road long ago inscribed in me.

Memory

The bike inscribes disconcerting things in you. Your seat has a memory that shouldn't be confused with ordinary memory. The body retains memories of episodes of effort. Sometimes the most difficult, most arduous memories are lost. What's left are unexpected memories of unexpected moments that at the time were not felt to be exceptional but which the muscles have chosen to remember for reasons of their own.

One day we came down from Saint-Véran, and we were caught in a storm at the bottom of the Guil valley, a classic mountain storm that pelted hard and dumped a lot of water. We had to stop at a café to wait. After a half hour most of the storm had passed, the heavy flow of water had drained from the road, and a fine rain had settled in. It wasn't very appealing, but it was rideable. So I volunteered to go get the car, which was parked in Guillestre. Those twenty kilometers in the rain are inscribed forever in my memory. They regularly come back up and speak to me of the bike. Was it the rain? Or the light that gradually came back, illuminating the road? Was it the mild descent that let me spin easily, in big gears? Or the bit of rest I had just had? I'll never know, because my muscles play back the rough memory in its intensity and length but without analysis.

The Austrian skier Franz Klammer once reenacted, in front of a movie camera, his winning run at Kitzbühel. He did it behind his businessman's desk, wearing a tie, his eyes closed, his hands in front of his face, tracing out the curves – and he did it in the same time, give or take a few seconds.

Through effort, something, perhaps contradictory, registers in you. At one spot between Yssingeaux and Retournac, the road, descending toward the valley of the Loire, abruptly goes up again for two hundred or three hundred meters. I hate these leg-breakers that glue you onto the road and get you revved up but don't let you really get into it or get into a climbing rhythm.

Still, it's that damned rise that'll come back up through my quads on the most minor occasion, and it doesn't come back up as a painful memory but rather as an incitement to accelerate. No doubt it's the terrible 'braking effect' that gives it the opposite virtue.

Friends

When we take off, side by side, in the early morning, we have so much to say to each other. We haven't seen each other since the day before, a week before, a year before, but soon we're breathing together, talking together.

For warming up there's nothing like conversation. The pedaling rhythm that allows for chatting is the ideal one for getting going. Clearly it varies from person to person, and seeing racers shooting the breeze at forty kilometers an hour, their hands on the top of the bars, gives the casual rider pause, but the principle is the same. As long as you talk while pedaling, you warm up gently. We talk about everything: books, movies, restaurants, work, life in general, the bike in particular.

I have cycling friends I see only on the bike – I wouldn't recognize them in a suit and tie. I have cycling friends I see all the time. We're a gang, a little *peloton*, a breakaway with variable geometry. Some mornings there are two of us, on others twelve, lost in an ocean of four thousand cyclists.

A group of buddies on bikes is almost always a group at the same level. You have to be in physical complicity to ride really well together. It's not a question of everyone being the same or having equal strength; it's just that each person has to contribute something to the group.

Cycling personalities are very well defined. As in the theater, biking has its types: it clearly reveals character and morphology, and what the casual observer notes among the racers is reproduced exactly among amateurs. Cycling has its bruisers and its scrawnies (the 'thigh guys' and the 'chicken calves,' as Jean-Noël Blanc would say); it's not particular about its morphotypes. Everyone has his chance.

If you consider climbers, for example, there are clearly two kinds: the angels, who are as big as minnows and who seem to be sucked up to the summits, and the bulls, who fight it out with gravity, with a great show of power and will. In the first category there's Charly Gaul and Pantani, in the second Hinault and Indurain. Each is capable of getting the better of the other so long as he stays in the realm of his own abilities: the bulls can't hope to follow the angels in their takeoffs, and the angels mustn't allow themselves to be stifled by the regular rhythm of the bulls. You have to know yourself.

These larger types are found among weekend riders, and you need this kind of diversity for a good group. Everyone needs to be able to put the screws to everyone else, and, in all circumstances, keep up, even with gritted teeth. Someone who's too fast won't help anyone develop and will get worn out waiting at the tops of climbs. Someone too slow will get sick of being a tagalong fool. The small groups of cyclists I've been involved with found a natural equilibrium through their deeper objective, which is to have a ball riding together.

The real fun happens in different ways. First of all, it's the pleasure of sharing nice things on the bike – things seen and felt, the effort, the heat. It's also the common desire to leave, to get out; alone maybe you'd stay in bed, figure out things to do, hesitate under a threatening sky. It's also the happiness of pulling out all the stops, like a bunch of kids. Speeding up 'just to see' is in the cyclist's nature. The essence of the bike lies in the freedom of racing. Even by myself I'll pull out all the stops. If I feel good, I step on it. If I still feel good, I step on it even more, until I don't feel so good. That's how I end up with a 'bust' (that's what they call a brief moment of tiredness, the kind that catches up with you at the end of the day).

One rider's brief acceleration, followed by others, are a gift to your conditioning – if you can follow. They make you better, even if you're frustrated when you're pushed hard – for me, this kind of frustration never lasts more than five seconds. It's discipline. I used to ski with Rémy, and we got along well. So I made the effort to convert him to cycling, and he became an impeccable cyclist – since you can take to biking at any age. Friends in life who are bike friends are double friends: soup and sandwiches.

The Others

You can ride long and far. Very quickly, with a good cycling technique and a little training, the body gets used to the effort and asks for more. After a few hundred kilometers you can pedal peacefully all day and consider taking on serious climbs and uneven terrain. After several hundred more, you can have fun accelerating and taking turns at the front. In this way you serenely arrive in the Eden known as 'being in shape.' So you think you're in paradise.

That's when, on your usual little route, on a climb, you hook up with another rider and you decide to stay on his wheel. In one single moment you lose your paradise, you lose your native tongue.

Hell is the rhythm of others.

When the decision to speed up or slow down is no longer yours, you become another cyclist. Through a kind of rebellious logic, it's always when your legs are tired that the rhythm speeds up, it's always when you're in the process of putting on your gloves that you have to get a move on . . . You experience, on a small scale, the difficulty of bike racing.

It's always in one's interest to know one's cycling buddies well, if you don't want to end up off the back. Sunday mornings, in the valley of the Chevreuse, I know that Rémy will accelerate on every climb. I know Rino will punish our legs on the flat at the top. I know Sébastien will never let up and that he'll always push himself beyond what he's capable of. That's how they're made, and how their souls have shaped their legs. You have to live with it.

When I was following the Tour de France, I saw professional racers, in the morning, livid with the thought that they might not be able to keep up with the pace of the *peloton*. I saw them again in the evening, worn out but happy to have been able to hang on to their place deep in the pack and to still be in the Tour.

We're so busy watching the head of the pack that we don't see the dignity and the honor involved in simply being there, in the rhythm of the others. The rhythm of the best, the rhythm of those who are strong for ten minutes, the rhythm of the warriors.

Racers feel very strongly the need for others, in order to train. That's exactly what they mean when they admit they're 'lacking competition.'

The others, whoever they are, make you pass another boundary in your knowledge of yourself, and in your conditioning. You were good, and thanks to them, now you're even better. Soon it will be up to you to impose *your* rhythm.

Spinning Circles

Blue Jersey

Taking advantage of the fact that I was wearing a blue jersey like the Italian team, I slipped into the Tour de l'Avenir. The strong guys had gone past some time before, and I picked out a big blond rider in a red jersey who was going up the pass at an acceptable pace.

I got behind him, then beside him, and we went up the Forclaz pass together, urged on by hordes of spectators.

He was Russian, and since I could stammer a bit in his language, we were able to exchange a few panted remarks. Above all he wanted to know if this hell was going to last much longer, if he still had to spend more hours scaling this infinite mountain, climbing beside those low white walls that line the route and reflect the sun's heat and light. He wanted water, which I gave him; he wanted his native Peace Race and its flat stages, and the central Asian plains. A little more and he would have sent me into a major-league depression while climbing hell-for-leather up to Chamonix.

For my part I was happy to be in the race and to knock down a few kilometers in good company. I carefully avoided mentioning the

Galibier, which he was going to have to climb the next day. We went up at a steady pace, and I took my share of pulls. I was happy to be in the Tour de l'Avenir – I was the right age. So I was able to dream in Russian for ten kilometers; then a motorcyclist came up to ask where my number was, and my career as clandestine passenger on board the race was over.

I said, 'Do svidania, tovarich,' and let my teammate go. By then he was only two kilometers from the summit.

Racer

For a long time I wondered why I wasn't a racer. Above all when I was in shape and riding fast. I don't have an exceptional physiology, but it's good enough. I could, perhaps, have been a racer in the ranks, at least racing.

One thing for sure: I could have tried.

I didn't do it.

The objective reasons are many: I had 'better things' to do, and at the age when one tries to become a racer, I had set off on other adventures. In the 1960s, sports and cycling in particular paid badly and were discouraging. Today it would be a different story. Sports are an excellent way to slip gloriously into traffic.

It was also the mood of the times. The preferred sport of my high-school friends was exemption from gym. Just about anything was good for nibbling away at those four unfortunate hours of weekly exercise and for transforming them into heavy study hours. The most clever guys, with help from their parents, found fantastic excuses, inflicting colds and chronic sore throats on themselves, so they could give math the time scheduled for muscles and play. So it was normal that athletes were seen as morons . . . For me, who liked sports as much as I liked studying, the pressure mounted a little more each time: how many times, when I was in preparatory classes for the École Normale, did I realize I was alone under the basketball hoop? How many solitary laps, in the courtyard of the high school, did I inflict on myself?

Like any self-respecting cheater, I slipped forbidden reading matter under my desk lid: *L'Équipe*, folded in eighths, just fit into the space between my books and notebooks and shattered the silence of the class with the racket of crumpled paper. I should be clear on this: I was hiding my reading from my classmates, not my teacher – he suffered from the same virus I had.

This secret muscle garden I tended so carefully every Sunday morning on my bike naturally marked me as a member of the moron clan. I was double, and it's hard to be a racer by halves.

There was also, and from the beginning, a little worm in the apple. I had the confused feeling of not liking the same cycling as my friends who were doing races. It wasn't a question of ethics or aesthetics – I never got involved in the ancient battle between touring cyclists and racers. Simply by instinct I felt closer to the latter. I pedaled like they did, I fought it out like they did, I collapsed like they did, and I had no great passion for the reasonable reason and the obligatory regularity of Audax rides. Still I didn't quite like the same cycling. I would have had a hard time saying why.

It was only in 1996, when I had the chance to follow the Tour and meet the champions, that I understood why I never raced. One finds, among former racers, the greatest haters of cycling. They can even tenaciously hate it, blaming it for their failures and doubts.

When I was able to talk with them about it, some told me simply that they were so sick of cycling at the end of their careers that the first thing they wanted to do was forget about it . . . Still they showed up at the Tour de France . . . 'for the ambiance,' they said. Others told me their job had nothing to do with bikes: it consisted of winning races, and 'going for rides' had no place in their future. Once they had retired from racing, bikes were useless.

A number of them also confessed that doping had convinced them to take a long break and seriously clean themselves up, and that they had lost their taste for cycling.

Former racers are also melancholy cyclists. They've lost their good feelings (both natural and artificial), and the Sunday cyclists with whom they could share a peaceful retirement upset them by always wanting to compete. As if a champion on one given day always has to be the champion! That ruins the very act of pedaling.

I remember the aged and pathetic Louison Bobet, who demanded that we – the kids – stay behind him on the Longchamp climb.

*   *   *

I'm sure I need the bike more than I need victories. I'd like to grow old as a cyclist. In ten, twenty years I'd still like to go out for a spin with Jean-Noël, with Rémy, with Sébastien.

Already I don't go as fast as before, but since I threw my speed to the four winds and never transformed it into bouquets or checks, it still lurks in the air of the mountains, and I breathe it in like an old perfume.

Doping

Some of the guys who raced in my area were in the habit of going to obscure dispensaries to improve their performance. One day I went along with two friends who were supposed to race in a time trial on the Forez plain. The race was on a circuit of about forty kilometers, and the starting line also served as the finish line. So it was a perfect circle, and they were hoping that the best riders could do it in less than an hour.

An oddball we knew, who had no other goal in life than to ride faster than his local friends, took off like a shot and crossed the line going the other way barely ten minutes later.

Everyone was waving his arms around, trying to get him to show some common sense, but he didn't see any problems. He came over to me, got off his bike, and told me: 'I think my time was good.'

We had to hide him for a few hours in the back seat of a Citroën to keep official eyes from seeing the foam dripping from his lips and to give him a chance to calm down.

As they used to say, 'he'd even swallowed the box.'

*   *   *

I've got nothing against doping – the problem's more complex than a simple pro or con game. I simply never had any desire to go down that road. Even if the effect of amphetamines on muscular power is negligible, their psychological effect on those who don't take them can be considerable.

It's commonly said that racers dope because it's a hard sport, but their sport is also hard precisely because they dope. The milieu of racers is a doper's milieu, and the serpent of doping endlessly bites its own tail. The lie is too old, and the hypocritical abyss they've allowed to open between the official line and real practices is too enormous ever to be done away with.

In the *peloton*, refusing to dope means refusing to 'do the job'; it's like refusing to train or get a massage.

Athletes have doped from day one. When the world was magical, dope was magical; when the world was chemical, dope was chemical; now that the world is biological, dope is biological; when, in the future, the world will be genetic, dope will be genetic: swimmers will have scales and cyclists will be born with saddles between their legs.

Doping itself has become a form of high-level competitive sport. They should do dope checks on the docs.

During the last Olympic games, in the same Arab country, at the same time, and in the same papers, you could read about the disqualification of three doping weightlifters and the protest of the sports organizations that were complaining that modern doping was a privilege of rich countries!

At the entry to the locker room of the gym in California where I used to work out, there was a permanent notice warning the public of the dangers associated with the use of anabolic steroids . . . which were for sale to anyone at the counter on the ground floor. Whole pages of the local paper sang the praises of growth hormones banned by the International Olympic Committee.

Competition produces doping, just as taxes produce fraud. What's annoying is that while the effects and injustices of doping are well known, it often takes a long time to figure out its forms.

To go dancing on Saturday night the younger generation nowadays takes the drugs Coppi used to win the Tour de France, and some racers who are nostalgic for the good old days can't train without a shot of grandpa's stuff in their popos. Without that it's a sad party and a gray road.

Cycle-Thoughts

Every year when I'm in France, we organize, on the occasion of the Saint-Étienne Book Festival, a hill climb with Jacques Plaine (I know – it's not his fault), who's the master of the proceedings and who rides a bike when he's not running marathons.

This race, which they've christened the Autumn Suns Climb, and which takes place, depending on the year, in the rain, the wind, the snow, and sometimes even in the sun, has become a great get-together. On the line there are writers, artists, former champions, kids from the local cycling school, and old old timers. I've seen Pierre Béarn, at the age of ninety-four, start off, tangling with those new-fangled gadgets, toe-clips.

Jacques Plaine has chosen the Pilat climb up to the Croix de Chaubouret as the route; I'm not too crazy about the course profile. It's true that since the idea is to climb it cold with the spigot wide open, there's little time left for savoring things. Nevertheless, it's a very uneven course, and it hurts your legs.

Once the clock has stopped at the summit, the game consists of coming back down, from village to village, from prize wine to hot wine, from sausages to tarts, finally arriving in town in a euphony indifferent to the brisk air and the occasional snowflake.

My friend Yvette had the good idea of absent-mindedly asking me to write a short article for *Le Progrès* on the occasion of each running of the race. For technical reasons this article has to be submitted at 1:00 P.M. Given the time needed for racing plus the time for showering and putting on a clean shirt, I'm forced to write it on the climb itself.

There are a lot of walker-poets, who write their verses to the rhythm of their feet: the Rédas, the Roubauds. Cyclist-poets are less numerous, it seems, but that's due to inattentiveness, since the bike is a good place to work for a writer. First, he can sit down; then he's surrounded by windy silence, which airs out the brain and is favorable to meditation; finally, he produces with his legs a fair number of different rhythms, which are so much music to verse and prose.

The difficulty, however, lies in the fact that on the Autumn Suns Climb, I try to climb quickly while writing. I'm short of breath, and my prose is choppy. I suffer from reduced lucidity, and my position keeps me from seeing everything. I'm a deaf, blind, and out-of-breath reporter.

Peaceful ramble days are perfect for text brewing. I leave with a sentence, an idea, and I spin it around for a few hours. I've come home with a story almost finished, an article, the end of a piece.

When I write this way, I can tell whether it's headwind prose or tailwind prose.

On a bike, I love working with paradoxical thoughts, thoughts that appear maladapted. Thinking methodically about Proust, about Queneau, for example, about Calder, about Howard Hawks; reciting *Le Pélican de Jonathan* by Jacques Roubaud; reconstructing *What a Man* by Georges Perec and *Oh l'ostrogoth* by Jacques Jouet. I love experimenting with the distortions that effort causes texts and reflections to undergo. What the open air brings to them. What sweat oxidizes in them. What they bring to my cycling performance.

These are displaced thoughts, and I can never know precisely whether their methodical exercise influences the steadiness of my pedaling or the steadiness of my pedaling influences the methodical side of my reflection.

Often these thoughts will be crazier, freer, than they would be in a living room. Less presentable too, sometimes pitted, sometimes shaken by sudden accelerations, unforeseen shortcuts, surprise breakaways. They have nothing to do with the chitchat topics I might share with my cycling friends: these are the thoughts and exercises of a solitary cyclist. On occasion they've served as preparation for writing.

I can't determine precisely the instant in which my thought escapes its object to become a thought of pure effort. The moment the rhythm speeds up, the moment the slope becomes steep, the moment fatigue gets the upper hand, thought doesn't fade away before the 'animal spirits;' on the contrary, it's reinforced and diffused throughout my entire body, becoming thigh-thought, back-intelligence, calfwit. This unconscious transformation is beyond me, and I only become aware of it much later, when the lion's share of the effort is over and thought flows back, returning to what is ordinarily considered its place.

Psy

It seems to me that if I had a psychoanalyst I'd nevertheless talk to him about the little obsessive phrases dictated by the rhythm, which can chase you for the length of a ride. About those songs that tend to reverberate all morning. About those obscure thoughts you ruminate on and that are turned into purée thanks to all the angry pedal strokes. I'd talk to him about it.

At the Table

I feel the need to be hungry. A real physical hunger, a simple desire to devour.

The bike hollows you out. For a gourmand it's a blessing. The quantity of energy expended is such that when evening comes around, you feel a pit in your stomach that seems unfillable. That kind of hunger is not to be found in the panoply of the sedentary person; it's a profound happiness he'll never feel.

For the cyclist there are two types of meals and two types of appetite: during and after.

During the effort, eating is a complex problem. One has to indulge in things that are high-calorie, light, quickly chewed, quickly swallowed, quickly digested. 'Eat before getting hungry,' Paul de Vivie advised, and he was right.

Wanting to do the right thing, and certainly guided by the memory of the contents of the old-time racers' musette bags, riders often set off with a chicken drumstick, a gooey-fruited tart, a leftover bit of steak, a ham sandwich, just to make sure they're not hungry at dinnertime. Hunger exists, but effort conceals it, and the prospect of swallowing a chicken thigh while pedaling up an inviting false flat is enough to make you heave.

There are yet deeper mysteries. I can't think of anything better than chocolate. I eat it upon getting up in the morning and every time I come across it during the day. I like it dark, dry, and hard. But I've never been able to eat a bit of it on the bike. The bike eliminates my taste for chocolate by turning it into a sticky, nauseating goo. No doubt I should see this as a nice lesson in the nonconcurrence of pleasures. One voluptuous delight at a time.

The effect of marzipan is the opposite; I don't like it, but on a bike it's a blessing.

The mounted cyclist is a different person.

When he's a pedestrian the cyclist once again is an ordinary gourmand but with a huge hole in his stomach – *peloton* hunger. So the custom quickly emerged, among *pelotons* and Sunday *gruppetti*, of putting finish lines at the entrances to good inns and of giving the winners nicely garnished bouquets.

I'm a fervent partisan of this custom, which renews the reputations of the classics. So I have very pleasant memories of a Paris-Troisgros through the Morvan, of an Arles-Bras via Mount Aigoual, of a Saint-Étienne–Loiseau through Burgundy, of a Paris-Gagnaire through the hills of the Forez, of a Saint-Étienne–Tournaire through the gorges of the Loire.

The prospect of a perfect dinner can make pedaling a delight. The Troisgros salmon scallop with sorrel, waiting at Roanne, is a real carrot, dangling in front of your nose. Riding along the Cévennes mountain road, you can hear the gurgling boiling of Laguiole vegetables. Around Beauzac, where the road goes above the valley of the Loire, you can already smell the green lentils of Puy, done in Tournaire style.

Everything is a celebration after eight hours of riding. The simplest things – the gratin Dauphinois, bolted down at the foot of the Iseran; spaghetti after climbing the Vars; Wiener schnitzel in the evening, after the Grossglockner.

A few years ago my father and I were riding in the Tyrol, and when we stopped, he was overcome by an insane desire for beer. Beer, which I practically never drink, is a great drink for the Sunday cyclist; it quenches your thirst, it's full of carbs, and it gives you a slight buzz that does away with your sore legs and stiff neck. Ordinarily it blows you up, Mongolfière style, but when you're suffering from cyclist's thirst it's like water from the spring.

My father, then, wanted some draught beer. In his broken German he ordered one, and they gave him a bottle. He drank it and ordered 'another beer,' a 'different one,' and he was cheerfully given a bottle of dark, which he drank unenthusiastically. Then he repeated his demand, and the dumbfounded innkeeper finally brought him his draught. These beers all came in the Austrian half-liter, and that series of three, even in Austria, made an impression. No – my father wasn't a drunk; he was just a cyclist.

*   *   *

One morning when I was going from Paris to Saint-Étienne, having gotten up very early, I decided to have my little snack break around ten o'clock. At that point I happened to be in the *département* of Cher, precisely in the small village of Apremont – an old village stretching along the Allier canal, watched over by the Schneider château, and kept up in all its former glory. A few Ks from there René Fallet did his cycling thing (among other things).

So I stopped at the auberge and ordered some fresh bread, hard-as-rock goat cheese, and a glass of Sancerre. It was nice and hot, and I was happy to have already knocked down a hundred kilometers and to be able to stick out my pins in the sun. The clientele touched their caps, looked at my bike, had a coffee, and went on their way to work, wordlessly. When, half-choked by the cheese, I asked the bar-lady to refill my glass, she objected – 'Don't even think about it! You're riding a bike. If you get drunk, you're going to risk your life.'

She was gracious enough not to talk about others' lives – so true it is that cyclists are gentle beings who rarely harm their neighbors. When I showed her I had only water in my bottles, she granted me a second glass – but didn't come back.

Fatigue

I feel the physical need for fatigue. More precisely, the refined range of kinds of fatigue. For just as there exist a hundred ways of feeling good on a bike, there are a hundred ways of being tired.

The fatigue I like best is that of trips in stages. When I've pedaled all day, fatigue hits me as soon my feet touch the ground. It accompanies me throughout the evening and into the night. It's both general and local: sore thighs, sore back.

In the morning I'm completely stiff, a rusty old wreck; I have trouble getting down the stairs. Without strength or desire I get on my bike, and pedal like an old robot.

Ten kilometers later, that's all gone. I feel fine. I even feel better than the day before – repeating the effort improves your conditioning and makes you sharper.

One summer I was coming down into Saint-Étienne with Rémy when I noticed that every morning we were quiet for about fifteen minutes. No doubt the cyclist's tongue – a fine muscle – also has its morning stiffness. That was the amount of time necessary for over-coming the fatigue and turning us back into chatterboxes. That kind of fatigue is good, it's cooperative.

On the other hand, you have to be careful about the fatigue that settles in and very quickly and very sneakily finds a way of expressing itself. It chooses a shoulder, the crotch, a tendon, and it locks itself in. From that point on magic creams won't work.

The only thing you can do then is go back to being a pedestrian.

After a year of intense work, I left Paris a little too hastily, without preparation, heading south – just to get out of prison. I was counting on my old 'skill' to take care of my lack of fitness. The first day was peaceful and soothing. The second morning a barely perceptible *click* settled into my left knee. As the day progressed it became a big *click*, and then a big knee.

So I had to end my excursion on the train, hugging my pretty bike out of fear of seeing it hung like a common side of beef from a baggage-car hook, and from there I took to my bed.

I slept three days and nights. That good old left knee acted as an alarm bell, warning me of a profound fatigue, greater than the bike could ever hope to efface.

By remaining attentive to the messages your body sends, through exercise and in pleasure, you can take an elegant inner voyage on the bike. A lasting voyage, a permanent school, continuous retraining. The dialogue you establish with your thighs is a rich one that helps you set your limits, improve your endurance, tolerate pain, and recognize the intolerable.

I find it useful every day.

I always watch for bouts of melancholy, a deep and hidden (to me) trait of my soul, and I keep an eye out for any loss of desire. I know that if I succumb to depression, it will start with a breakdown in my thighs. It will start with cycling sluggishness, and the rest will follow.

Getting Old

Getting old with the bike means gaining endurance and wisdom. It's having the ability to go further more calmly, to train better, and, in general, to get more out of it.

But aging also means going slower, 'lunging' less quickly, soon not lunging at all, and soon not caring that somebody else lunges right in front of you.

There's ruin in the cyclist's aging as well. I rode the fastest between the ages of twenty-eight and thirty-two. Since then, I've been on the decline – and it's not going to get any better.

This decline, which happens in stages, is tolerable. You can manage it in the fatalistic mode, you can manage it in friendship – aging in the *peloton*. The only indispensable things are a real love of the bike and a reasonable serenity.

The big existential advantage of this aging of the thighs is that it always precedes the overall, inevitable aging of the cyclist himself.

Therefore I've entrusted my bike with the mission of notifying me of my aging. It's doing nicely.

Blowup

Extreme cycling fatigue is very distinctive. 'Blow up,' 'fall flat,' 'do a nose dive' are expressions that have clear enough derivations. This extreme fatigue is symbolized well by a character who's famous in all the world's *pelotons*: he goes by the moniker 'The Man with the Hammer.'

The Man with the Hammer is hidden behind a turn (you don't know which one), and he's waiting for you. When you go by, with sprightly legs, he smashes his big old hammer on your neck and turns you into a wreck. Then, even if you were to say that you had seen his shadow for some time, stretched out on the road, no one would believe you.

You can't anticipate this kind of fatigue. It appears suddenly, and it is terrible. You'd sell your soul to get rid of it.

My life as a rider is a collection of nosedives – my own and others'.

I've seen my brother-in-law, Jacques, who's a hell of a rider, sitting in the ditch on the north face of the Ventoux, three hundred meters from the top, absolutely refusing to finish the climb. I've seen myself going up the Béal pass, zigzagging, with Jean-Loup, having forgotten my name, looking for a way out. I've seen my father abandon me, when I wasn't ten years old, on the one-hundred-kilometer Vélocio ride, letting me ride on with a packet of Beurre-Lu cookies as my only provisions.

The worst thing to do in such cases is to rest 'just a bit' before setting off again. The second you get back on your bike the fatigue immediately returns, massively, with its yoke of pain.

It's too late. Anything that could do you good – drinking, eating, stretching out – nauseates you. You'd offer your bike to the first passerby so as not to see it again. The smidgen of thought left in your brain is a profound sense of the absurd, which makes you want to vomit.

Your sweat is like ice, your skin is pallid, and you curl into a ball on the embankment. Your entire body is in revolt.

With experience you get the feeling you can master these blowups. It's not true. But you get to know them. You know that you'll get out of it, you panic less, and you recover quicker.

I think the origins of doping can be found in the specific character, and the suddenness, of this kind of fatigue.

Blowups in races are measured in lost quarter hours and lost races. They're easy enough to spot. In a few seconds, champions can age ten years, their faces hollow, their eyes sunken. The great Eddy Merckx, at the moment Bernard Thévenet caught up with him on the climb to Pra-Loup, was ready for a deck chair.

It seems there's something you don't know about that's brewing inside you. A big black lump that was forming in your chest, while you were peacefully pedaling. There are warning signs of a blowup, but they aren't appreciably different from the signs of normal tiredness. Now that I think about it, metaphysical anxiety might be one hint.

Riding is absurd – climbing to descend, going in circles, behind this mountain there's another, why hurry? . . . Riding is absurd, like peeling vegetables, skiing, thinking deeply, or living. The moment these questions come up, while you're riding, you should take note. That's when your quads are demanding more oxygen from your heart than your lungs can provide. That's when it gets foggy. If you're on a friend's wheel, he'll pull away by two bike-lengths without accelerating. You come back, dancing on your pedals, but then you lose the two lengths again. You do this rubber-band trick ten or so times, and then you let him go, telling yourself you'll catch up soon. In fact, the next time you see him is when he turns around and comes back, worried, to find out what happened. At that point you won't recognize him, or, better yet, you'll recognize him, but only as someone who might buy your disgusting bike.

One day, around four in the afternoon, I was riding alone and took a terrible nosedive; I decided to go straight to the next hotel. I was such a perfect grouch – wanting them to open the garage, demanding a room on the ground floor (ah, the idea of going up one floor!), refusing to fill out the forms – that the staff started to get irritated. Lucky for me, the owner was a cyclist. 'Leave him alone, he's cooked,' he said. And he took charge of things, giving me a little break for two or three hours to let me come back to reality.

Every blowup is a furious descent deep into oneself, into murky regions where things seem to knot up incessantly.

Why not give up the bike after a blowup?

Because the blowup is a journey, and the cyclist is first and foremost a traveler.

Then because, after a blowup, your organism is altered. There's a kind of purification in falling flat, an impression of fasting. A threshold is crossed that brings you closer to being in shape – the next day, when the worst of the tiredness is over, you feel it. To such an extent that some racers include a blowup in their training. I remember Fignon, three days before the world championships, setting off to do three hundred kilometers alone, with a cereal bar. He went out to meet the Man with the Hammer.

If Fignon needs it, just about any clown, like me, can use a blowup too.

In Shape

The profound truth of the need for fatigue, its end, is the need for fitness.

Nonathletes should, at least once in their lives, indulge in the luxury of being in shape. It's a physical experience that's worth the trouble.

Even after many years of activity it remains a mystery.

After the winter break (not all cyclists have the opportunity to spend winter in the sun), the first outings are laborious. They're dappled with small pains. Little chills, cramps, loss of desire. Still, there's steady improvement and you get your bearings again.

And then one morning you feel like you've been let out of prison. The air, the same as it was the day before, seems light; the countryside opens up, and you feel at home in the fold of the mountain. You like the hill you're climbing, and to celebrate you upshift two cogs and accelerate. You're in shape.

Nothing can get in your way, and you pedal delightedly.

*   *   *

Fitness is a global state applicable to all the facets of the bike. You pedal smoothly, as if in oil, you climb well, you descend quickly. You're capable of efforts that you yourself find astonishing. You're happy.

One summer, while I was staying in Bédoin, near my friend Bens, I decided to go and climb the Ventoux. I left around six, to avoid the intense heat. It was early morning and the birds were singing in the grapevines. No one was around, and because the air was still brisk, I developed a quick cadence on the flat part and on the false flat that comes before the steep section.

Arriving at the fateful left turn, which rises before you like a wall and which rather bluntly indicates the beginning of the serious stuff, I got into a lower gear but maintained the same cadence. I kept it to the top, wary of the blowup hiding behind every cork-oak, behind every bush, and then behind every rock – and it never came.

At the summit (even the long ledge at the end seemed gentler) I decided to take the road down to Malaucène.

At Malaucène, where it was already hot, rather than taking the road on the left, winding through the vines (Côtes de Ventoux, AOC) to Bédoin, I purely and simply turned around and treated myself to another Ventoux.

At noon, having showered and shaved, I was back with my friend Bens, watching the truffle-oaks grow in the field across the way.

Fitness is a climb. That's why riding in the high mountains is such a beautiful metaphor. The bad thing about climbs is that they have a summit. One day your fitness stops going up, and it starts to twist and turn. That's when the alternation between 'with' and 'without' days starts.

Their distribution can be surprising, and the Tour de France racers themselves told me that it was their first question of the day, their first worry. They flung themselves at rises in order to know whether they were, yes or no, silky smooth.

I have an urgent need for 'with' days.

Circles

The human body, which has such pretty curves, makes very few circles. You can certainly twiddle your thumbs, but that doesn't get you very far.

Riding a bike means going in circles. You have to think about it when you pedal, reminding yourself: your leg movement is circular, you have to grant it this, and turn the cranks roundly. Cyclists have an excellent sense of this, and as soon as the cadence falls, and fatigue mounts, they say they're 'pedaling squares.'

The cyclist is his own gyroscope. He produces not only movement but equilibrium. The faster he turns his legs, the more harmonious this equilibrium becomes: he's 'spinning.'

Spinning up a hill, for example, is being attached to a nylon cord that leads you up to the top. A cyclist's equilibrium is a circular equilibrium.

If your wheels spin round, your legs spin round; if your legs spin round, your head will too.

When something isn't spinning right, I pedal to go back up the line of good equilibrium, to get my gyroscope going again. Endowed deep down with a depressive nature, I build ramparts and fortresses of good humor and work; the bike is my essential metaphor, my fundamental model. As long as I'm pedaling, I'm in equilibrium; as long as I'm pedaling, I'm spinning circles.

To create a desire for something one needs is to engage in a labor of human happiness. Need is a demanding and obscure thing that defines the dependence of one person on another. To identify it and want it is to define oneself as a person. That's the secret of culture, the secret of cuisine, the secret of kindness. It's also the secret of tiny Fournel on his bike in the vast countryside, miraculously in equilibrium on his two wheels, trying to catch his own shadow.

From Cairo

In Cairo – where I've written a number of these pages – I've gone through, after forty-five years of continuous cycling, my first experience of cycling severance. I just don't see where I could slip a bike into this city, nor do I see, between the overburdened valley of the Nile and the deserted desert tracks, any shady countryside I could explore.

The Nile on a bike doesn't tempt me. The white and solitary desert is hardly amusing either – they'd find me melted in the minimal shade of some ruin. Strangely, the only cyclists I run into in the city ride with one hand. With the other they hold up a two-square-meter tray, balanced on their head, on which are placed two hundred loaves – round, puffy *baladis*, which are arranged in a pyramid (a mania) and sold for a few piasters on street corners. That's how they ride through the streets, their necks stiff, weaving among the cars, scanning with wary eyes, anticipating obstacles and stops with a sort of belly dance that enables the whole edifice to stay erect. If by chance a rider loses a loaf, he leaves it to the cars or to the children, who dive under wheels for the pleasure of a snack.

Arriving at the street corner where the soup vendor has set up his cans, the cyclist stops. Helping hands relieve him of his burden, and he sets off for another one, holding his handlebars with both hands.

I have trouble seeing myself recycled as a Cairine bread delivery-man. So I'm biding my time. My bike's wrapped up in the basement in Paris, ready to go. I stay seated and wait – heavy, immobile.

I'm watching my thighs melt and my belly get round. I write about the bike, alternately flexing my two legs under the table. I plan out routes in the desert; I read maps that show straight arid lines stretching for three hundred kilometers between oases. I ask myself where on my handlebars I could attach a compass and a GPS.

Not having a two-square-meter tray on my head, I'm trying to figure out how I could create my own shade.

At first, for the first few weeks, I didn't really notice I wasn't riding.

In fact – and I'm struck by this – it's very easy not to ride a bike. You hang around in bed an hour later on Sunday; you jump behind the wheel of the car without thinking; you look for a parking spot close to your office; your legs are never sore; that bit of soreness in your knee disappears. You hardly think about it. You don't see any cyclists in the streets (not 'real' ones); you don't come across any in the country; you don't see any bikes in shop windows. You forget. Your friends write that they went out on Sunday, and it seems further still.

That lasts for a few weeks.

And then one morning – the other morning – I felt blurry. I realized I didn't have any contours, any edges. I no longer knew exactly where my body stopped and space started. I could have gotten huge, or tiny to the point of disappearing, without noticing it. I lived, doubting like this, through that day and night, from time to time touching myself to make sure I really was soft.

At two in the morning my right calf, which is a real scold, cramped up terribly. We went for a little walk in the hallway, and taking advantage of our nocturnal intimacy, it let me know very clearly that the time had come to get back on the road.

Trying to cheat, I hobbled forth the next morning to flush out an health club – which I was unable to do.

So I'm waiting now for the moment when my calf, via the little secret wire that transmits short commands from my cycling brain ('take off,' 'slow down,' 'lay a patch'), will send back its violent message and start to pull my morale down into my socks. I have the feeling it'll manage to turn me into a huge captive ape, making me hate the neighborhoods and the landscapes, making me hate the whole country; that it'll plant in my mind the simple idea that the time has come to return to a country with pretty roads.

That's how my cycling calves operate: independent, with a will, and I've been cohabiting with them since that day in July when I was nine years old, and, riding my green dragon, on the wheel of the Baron, I attacked the climb to Pont-de-Lignon.

Breinigsville, PA USA
17 November 2010
249408BV00005B/2/P